Cruzan v. Missouri:

THE RIGHT TO DIE

SUPREME COURT MILESTONES

Cruzan v. Missouri:

THE RIGHT TO DIE

LILA PERL

Marshall Cavendish
Benchmark
New York

With special thanks to Professor David M. O'Brien of the Woodrow Wilson Department of Politics at the University of Virginia for reviewing the text of this book.

Marshall Cavendish Benchmark
99 White Plains Road
Tarrytown, NY 10591
www.marshallcavendish.us

Library of Congress Cataloging-in-Publication Data

Perl, Lila.
    Cruzan v. Missouri : the right to die / by Lila Perl.
      p. cm. — (Supreme Court milestones)
    Includes bibliographical references and index.
    ISBN-13: 978-0-7614-2581-6
    1. Cruzan, Nancy—Trials, litigation, etc. 2. Cruzan, Joe—Trials,
    litigation, etc. 3. Right to die—Law and legislation—United States.
    I. Title.
    KF228.C78P47 2007
    344.7304'197--dc22

                                             2006025740
Photo research by Connie Gardner

Cover Photo: Pixtail/SuperStock

The photographs in this book are used by permission and through the courtesy of:
SuperStock: Pixtail, 2–3; *Getty Images:* Keith Phillpot, 6, 12, 47, 79; Cynthia Johnson, 93; Mark Wilson, 95; Stringer, 102; Bob Schindler, 115; *Corbis:* 29; Reuters, 17; Bettmann, 32, 37, 39, 65, 71; Michael S. Lewis, 49; Carlos Barria, 113; *AP Photo:* Gene J. Puskar, 60; Adam Nadel, 86; Don Ryan, 98; Chris O'Meara, 106; Robert Sullivan, 109.

Publisher: Michelle Bisson
Art Director: Anahid Hamparian
Series Designer: Sonia Chaghatzbanian
Printed in China
1 3 5 6 4 2

contents

IN 1981, NANCY BETH CRUZAN WAS A HAPPY, HEALTHY, ENERGETIC YOUNG WOMAN. IN 1983, LIFE AS SHE HAD KNOWN IT WAS RADICALLY CHANGED BY AN AUTOMOBILE ACCIDENT THAT SENT HER SPINNING INTO A PERSISTENT VEGE-TATIVE STATE.

ON AN OCTOBER DAY IN 1987, a young lawyer named William Colby made his first visit to a young woman named Nancy Beth Cruzan, who had been lying comatose in a hospital bed for nearly five years.

One might ask why a lawyer rather than a doctor had undertaken to look in on Nancy and what purpose such a visit might serve. The answer soon became evident. As Bill Colby, accompanied by members of Nancy's family, approached her bed in a room on the fourth floor of the Missouri Rehabilitation Center, this is what he saw.

"Nancy's bloated face was pointed at the wall and was contorted into an unnatural grimace, its skin a chalky, sickly color, dotted with spots of red acne. Her eyes blinked every couple of seconds. Soft groans escaped from her mouth, as did a trickle of drool, which ran down her chin and onto the bedsheets. Her arms were pulled up almost like a boxer protecting his face, except, instead of fists, each of Nancy's wrists bent unnaturally back, with her fingers splayed. An embroidered pillow was wedged between her fingernails and the skin on the inside of her wrist—later I learned that the pillow stopped her nails from cutting into her skin."

Five years earlier Nancy Cruzan had been a lively,

outgoing young woman of twenty-five, married to her second husband, living and working in southwestern Missouri, and still very much a part of the family in which she'd grown up. Of the three daughters of Joe and Joyce Cruzan, Nancy, the eldest, was the one who seemed to enjoy life the most, was always bursting with energy, and was somehow the leader of the clan.

Then on the night of January 11, 1983, Nancy Cruzan apparently lost control of her car as she was driving alone on a dark country road. The car overturned and Nancy was thrown face down into a ditch at a considerable distance from the wreck. By the time emergency medical aid arrived and discovered the location of Nancy's body, she had no heartbeat and was not breathing.

Paramedics administered cardiopulmonary resuscitation (CPR) and her heart and lungs resumed functioning. But Nancy's brain had been irreparably damaged because brain cells begin to die within a few minutes of being deprived of oxygen. Six minutes without oxygen (a condition known as anoxia) would have been enough to cause permanent brain injury. In Nancy's case, she had ceased breathing for twelve to fourteen minutes, possibly longer.

Now, after nearly five years of being totally helpless, her body twisted and shrunken, Nancy was surviving only because (unable to eat normally) she was being given food and water via a tube that had been surgically inserted through her abdominal wall directly into her stomach. Nancy's husband and her father both had to give their signed permission for the hospital to perform the gastrostomy, the opening of a hole into her stomach through which the feeding tube would be implanted.

The other major requirement for keeping Nancy alive was almost hourly care to help with her eliminatory functions and to turn her body frequently so her skin would not develop bedsores and other lesions.

Although Nancy's eyes were open and she appeared to be experiencing cycles of sleeping and waking, she was unable to hear, speak, or respond to stimuli because the cells of the cerebral neocortex (the "thinking" part of her brain) had died. Her breathing, her heart action, and the occasional movements and sounds she made were the unconscious workings of the still-functioning brain stem.

In short, like some 14,000 other patients at any given time in the United States, Nancy was in what is known as a persistent vegetative state (PVS). With feeding and proper hygienic care, she could go on living for decades. The longest-lived PVS patient at the time, according to the *Guinness Book of World Records*, was a woman named Elaine Esposito, who lapsed into PVS following surgery in 1941 at the age of six and lived for thirty-seven years, dying at age 43 in 1978.

By 1986, almost four years after Joe and Joyce Cruzan's daughter had ceased to be the vibrant young woman they had once known, the Cruzan family began to seriously discuss asking the hospital to withdraw the feeding tube, so that Nancy could die a natural death. They felt that her hopeless condition and their own anguish should not be allowed to go on for decades. Moreover, they believed that this was the death that nature had intended for Nancy, and that would have taken place in the ditch by the roadside had she not received emergency CPR.

By this time, Nancy's husband, Paul Davis, had agreed to a divorce and drifted away, and Nancy's father, Joe Cruzan, had become her legal guardian. But when he petitioned the Missouri Rehabilitation Center to remove the feeding tube that he had agreed should be implanted—and that had never "rehabilitated" Nancy—he was refused on the ground that removing the tube would be the equivalent of starving her to death.

The Missouri Department of Health informed Joe

Cruzan that only "a specific Order of the Courts of Missouri" would lead the hospital to even consider such an unlikely action. It was at this point that Joe Cruzan began to seek legal advice and became the client of William Colby, the young Kansas City lawyer whose firm permitted him to work *pro bono publico* (for the good of the public) on the Nancy Beth Cruzan case.

During the three years that followed, Colby would lead the Cruzan quest for a right to die for Nancy through a labyrinth of courts that included three in Missouri. He would also argue Nancy's case in the highest court in the land, the U.S. Supreme Court.

The underlying issue would be, first, the question of whether there is a "right" to die that can be derived from the wording of the U.S. Constitution. Second, can such a right be determined by courts or legislative bodies, state or federal? Finally, is death preferable to survival under intolerable circumstances or must life be preserved regardless of its quality?

one
DO WE NEED A "RIGHT" TO DIE?

DEATH IS THE natural DESTINY of all living things. Human beings, however, are believed to be the only members of the animal species who are aware of death's inevitability. So it is not surprising that—especially in their later years—people should become increasingly concerned with death's many aspects. How many more years can I expect to live? What illness or accident, or possibly a combination of both, will be responsible for my demise? Will I suffer a prolonged period of pain or discomfort before dying, or will my death be painless, dignified, and peaceful?

On the other hand, we live in a society that regards death as a subject that is somehow taboo. This is also an age of highly advanced medical technology, in which we believe that there is a cure for almost anything that ails us or threatens to cut our lives short. As a result, we tend to deny the reality of death. We want to believe that life can always be prolonged, and that its extension is a good thing.

The plea of Nancy Cruzan's father to secure a court order from the state of Missouri to allow Nancy to have her feeding tube withdrawn, so that she might experience a natural death, tells us something else, however. It tells

JOE AND JOYCE CRUZAN BELIEVED THAT THEIR DAUGHTER NANCY SHOULD BE ALLOWED TO DIE A NATURAL DEATH. THE CRUZANS' BATTLE WENT ALL THE WAY TO THE U.S. SUPREME COURT.

us that there may be circumstances—such as the persistent vegetative state, or PVS—under which the artificial extension of life is not considered a good thing for the patient or her family.

A DETAILED LOOK AT PVS

The persistent vegetative state was first described in detail in 1972. Cases had, of course, existed before. But with the development of more rapid and effective CPR treatment and respirators that could be brought to the scene of an accident, doctors began to see an increase in PVS cases at about that time.

Ronald Cranford, M.D., a neurologist and medical ethicist who testified in the Cruzan case in the late 1980s, defined PVS as "a complete lack of consciousness." This was due to the fact that the neocortex (the "thinking" part of the brain) was more quickly damaged by lack of oxygen than the hardier brain stem, the primitive part of the brain that controls involuntary and unconscious reactions.

In Cranford's words, "There may be, and often are, facial movements and other signs indicating an apparent manifestation of conscious human suffering. . . . Families are often quite distressed by these subcortical and brain-stem reflex responses, which they mistakenly interpret as a conscious interaction with the environment and an indication that the patient is experiencing distress."

It is these primitive reflex actions such as grimaces, moans, and other throat sounds, blinking and even occasional tears that give vain hope for improvement and even recovery to the families and loved ones of PVS patients. Such families are also convinced that the withdrawal of artificially delivered food and water will cause painful sensations of thirst and starvation to the patient.

According to medical experts such as Cranford, pain and suffering can be felt only when a person's neocortex is intact and functioning. Although families of PVS patients, before and after Nancy Cruzan, did not accept this medical explanation of the condition, the Cruzans did and so pursued their efforts to have Nancy's feeding tube withdrawn.

The quest for a legally sanctioned "right" to die has also arisen from the anguish of patients afflicted with other immobilizing disabilities such as paralyzing strokes and spinal-cord injuries, as well as terminal diseases (those from which there can be no recovery).

AIDS (acquired immune deficiency disease) was first identified in 1982. Its ravages in the most full-blown cases have included severe joint pains, skin lesions, respiratory infections, fevers and sweats, and a wasting of the body that leaves it open to a deadly form of pneumonia.

Death came more quickly to AIDS patients before the introduction of combinations of drugs that, although they do not cure the disease, do prolong life. Yet, as their lives are extended, people with AIDS tend to develop a variety of cancerous conditions.

Chemotherapy and other cancer treatments are administered but these further weaken the already damaged immune systems of the sick.

As a result, AIDS patients have joined the ranks of those with cancer who clamor for the "right" to die due to pain, disfigurement, and a quality of life that has become insupportable.

Similarly, degenerative diseases such as ALS (Lou Gehrig's disease) and Alzheimer's often drive patients to seek a means of ending their lives. Amyotrophic lateral sclerosis (ALS) is a neuromuscular condition that causes the gradual deterioration of the body's mobility. It may start with the arms and legs, rendering them useless, and culminate with the inability to swallow so that the patient chokes on his or her own saliva.

Alzheimer's, a brain disease that leads to progressive mental deterioration, predominates among older members of the population. Victims, however, who are in the beginning stages, have been known to seek an early release from the disorientation and helplessness that lie ahead.

THE EUTHANASIA OF Dr. JACK KEVORKIAN

The word *euthanasia* is derived from the Greek words *eu* (good or easy) and *thanatos* (death). The English scholar and statesman, Sir Francis Bacon, coined this word in the early 1600s. Lingering and painful deaths, however, had plagued humanity from the beginning of time. Kevorkian began his campaign to provide death on demand in the 1980s, although only in cases he considered to be qualified. But he had long had an interest in the physical processes of death.

Kevorkian's "suicide machine," which he called the Mercitron, was designed to provide either a lethal injection or carbon monoxide poisoning via inhalation. Although Kevorkian set up the means of death, he did not physically operate the machine. Instead it was placed within the patient's reach so that, after being hooked up, the patient could push the button that would release the deadly substance.

Following the death of Janet Adkins, whose decision had had the approval of her husband, Kevorkian went on to provide a means of suicide to more than one hundred other patients. They suffered from such conditions as multiple sclerosis, ALS, cancer, emphysema, and congestive heart disease.

Kevorkian had often appeared on television and even gave the tape of a death he had provided to an ALS sufferer to CBS's *60 Minutes* television program. The showing of the tape, in November 1998, prompted the state of Michigan to charge Kevorkian with second-degree murder. He was convicted in 1999 and sentenced to serve a 10- to 25-year jail sentence.

In 1990, the public became acquainted with the case of an Oregon woman who sought physician-assisted suicide (PAS) outside the law after being diagnosed with Alzheimer's disease. Although the disease was still in its early stages, Janet Adkins, age fifty-four, whose wishes were well known in advance, became the first suicide of the notorious Jack Kevorkian. Kevorkian was a medical doctor with a Michigan license who, in 1988, had built a "suicide machine" for the purpose of providing voluntary euthanasia to those who sought it.

THE GROWTH OF THE "RIGHT"-TO-DIE MOVEMENT

While Jack Kevorkian's approach to voluntary euthanasia was openly defiant of the law and was intended to influence physicians elsewhere in the United States to provide some form of assisted suicide to their patients, others attempted to find a legal means of offering end-of-life solutions for the desperately ill.

As early as 1906, the state of Ohio attempted to draft the first euthanasia bill in the country. It would have allowed incurably ill or injured patients to request death in the presence of three witnesses. The effort failed.

Euthanasia societies were formed in England and in the United States in the 1930s but they appeared to be limited to the interests of their closest adherents. The subject of an inflicted death at the request of a patient was seen as close to suicide or murder, and was almost unanimously frowned upon by religious bodies, the government, and the medical profession.

The public was shocked when, in 1958, a book entitled *Death of a Man* was published in the United States. Author Lael Wertenbaker described how she had helped her husband to die to escape an incurable and painful illness. This book, however, turned out to be the first of a genre.

DR. JACK KEVORKIAN'S NAME BECAME SYNONYMOUS WITH THE "RIGHT-TO-DIE" MOVEMENT IN THE 1980S AND 1990S. IN 1999, KEVORKIAN WAS CONVICTED OF SECOND DEGREE MURDER FOR ASSISTING WITH A SUICIDE AND WAS SENTENCED TO 10 TO 25 YEARS IN PRISON.

Other titles followed, dealing with the desperation of terminally ill patients and of family members who complied with their wishes. Surprisingly, the writers of these works were not prosecuted, perhaps because specific statutes against such assisted deaths did not exist in the states in which they lived.

Foreign nations, too, reported cases of assisted suicide. In the Netherlands, in 1973, a woman name Geertruida Postma gave her elderly and dying mother a fatal injection at her request. Postma, who was also a physician, was charged with murder and found guilty.

But the cultural and religious views of the Dutch with regard to PAS have, in general, been broader and more liberal than those held in the United States. As a result, Postma was given a suspended sentence and a year's probation. Today, if physicians in the Netherlands follow the guidelines of the Royal Dutch Medical Association, they will not be prosecuted for PAS by the Dutch Supreme Court.

What were some of the factors that pushed Americans in the 1960s and the 1970s to seek legislation allowing a "right" to die in cases of terminal illness or, failing that, to take the law into their own hands?

Looking back to the first half of the twentieth century, we note that most people died in their own homes, as had been the case from earliest times. Starting in about 1950, however, about 50 percent of the U.S. population began dying in hospitals, nursing homes, or other medical institutions. By 1951, that percentage was up to 61 percent, and by 1978 to 71 percent.

Today 85 to 90 percent of Americans spend their final hours in hospitals or other medical settings, often hooked up to "beeping and squealing monitors, the hissing of respirators and pistoned mattresses, the flashing multicolored electronic signals—the whole technological panoply . . ."

These are the words of physician and author Sherwin

Nuland in his book, *How We Die*. Nuland laments the absence of "the tranquillity we have every right to hope for" and the fact that we are "separated from those few who would not let us die alone."

He points out that "By such means, biotechnology created to provide hope serves actually to take it away, and to leave our survivors bereft of the unshattered final memories that rightly belong to those who sit nearby as our days draw to a close."

It is certainly true that the discovery of antibiotics such as penicillin to fight deadly infections and ventilators that breathe for us have prolonged life. Additionally, we have benefited from sophisticated diagnostic tests such as CAT (computer axial tomography) scans and MRIs (magnetic resonance imaging).

Constantly improving surgical techniques, and the newest and most effective means of dealing with the failure of vital organs such as the heart, lungs, and kidneys are now with us. Advanced chemotherapy and radiation treatments are available for cancer, and there are new and more effective drugs to fight AIDS.

Even with every technological medical marvel of the age, however, we cannot cure all human ills and often succeed merely in prolonging the dying process under conditions of duress for both patients and their families.

At the same time that medical advances were extending life for the very sick, a series of rights movements were taking shape and expanding in the United States. During the 1960s and 1970s, they included the civil rights movement for fair and equal economic, social, and political opportunities for African Americans and other minorities.

The women's rights movement became strong and influential and, in 1973, the U.S. Supreme Court decision in the *Roe* v. *Wade* case gave women the right to choose lawful medical abortion if they so desired. During this period, student rebellions seethed in support of these and other human rights issues.

The right that appeared to be the most instrumental in establishing legal access to abortion was the right of privacy, which the Court interpreted to be derived from parts of the U.S. Constitution, including the Fifth and Fourteenth Amendments, among others. Could this right apply to death as well as birth? In other words, if individual citizens had a fundamental right to make their own decisions about marriage and family size, why could they not also make choices about the conditions under which they chose to live or die in the final weeks or months of life?

Not surprisingly, it was during the period of the rights ferment that the first so-called Living Will was presented to the American public. It was written by an attorney named Louis Kutner, who published it in the *Indiana Law Review* in the summer of 1969.

The Living Will was a document by means of which an adult individual who was still healthy and competent could indicate the kind and extent of treatment wanted or not wanted in the event of becoming unable to make his or her wishes known.

Kutner's argument for the establishment of Living Will laws was based on the fact that "the current state of the law does not recognize the right of the victim to die if he so desires. He may be in a terminal state of suffering from an incurable illness and literally forced to continue a life of pain and despair. Such a denial may well infringe upon an individual's right of privacy."

Although the adoption of Living Will laws in the United States was relatively slow at first, by 1984 twenty-two states and the District of Columbia had laws that recognized the use of these so-called advance care directives. (Missouri was not one of them.) Today the use of both Health Care

Proxies (also known as Medical Power of Attorney or Durable Power of Attorney for Health Care) and Living Wills is almost universal in the United States, and an overwhelming majority of Americans approve their use.

The Health Care Proxy and the Living Will differ in the following ways. The former empowers another person or persons of the individual's choosing (usually a family member or trusted friend) to make health care decisions in the event that the patient is unable to do so. The latter spells out the medical treatment that the patient desires or refuses under specific conditions.

The introduction of the Living Will concept in 1969 was followed in 1973 by a twelve-point document issued by the American Hospital Association called the Patient Bill of Rights. Ideals expressed in the new patients' rights literature included "considerate and respectful care" on the part of medical and hospital staff, as well as regard for truth, confidentiality, and privacy in dealing with patients.

Patients were to be thoroughly informed before being asked to consent to treatment and they were to have the right "to refuse treatment to the extent permitted by law." As to right-to-die policies, they were, as they still are today, controlled mainly by the individual states.

It would take many years for patients' rights regarding informed consent and the right to refuse treatment in nonterminal cases to be recognized and accepted by some elements of the hospital and medical profession. Meantime, terminally ill patients faced another big problem: the poor end-of-life care that was available either in hospitals or at home.

END-OF-LIFE CARE AND THE HOSPICE MOVEMENT

The 1960s and 1970s, the period of the individual and civil rights movement, also gave rise to a new concept in

A LOOK aт a LIVIПG WILL

Although formats vary from state to state, an example of the wording of a Living Will in the state of New York is as follows:

In the event that I am unable to make health care decisions for myself, my wishes are as follows:

(1) Medication and treatment should not be or continue to be administered to me for therapeutic purposes or to prolong my life if:

(a) I have an incurable or irreversible condition that is likely to cause my death within a relatively short time, or

(b) I am in a state of permanent unconsciousness or a persistent vegetative state, or

(c) I am conscious but have irreversible brain damage and it is likely that I will never regain the ability to make decisions and express my wishes, or

(d) It is likely that I will never again live without the aid of mechanical respiration or without artificial nutrition and hydration, or

(e) I have an incurable or irreversible condition which is not terminal but which causes me to experience severe and progressive physical or mental deterioration and loss of capacities I value, so that the burdens of continued life (with treatment) are greater than the benefits I experience.

The Living Will goes on to ensure that the conditions described above are determined by a physician and cites that under those circumstances the patient does not want mechanical respiration, cardiopulmonary resuscitation, or artificial nutrition and hydration, but does want to be as free of pain as possible.

A Living Will may state that the patient prefers to live out his or her last days at home rather than in a hospital, if feasible, even though this may, along with pain medication, shorten the period of life that is left. Other special requests may be added, and placed in the hands of the patient's health care proxy to be carried out.

The Living Will can be revoked or changed at any time before a disabling illness or accident strikes.

end-of-life care. Did not the dying have a right to end their days in an atmosphere free of the tubes, monitors, ventilators, and other medical paraphernalia that could not save them, but could and did prolong their discomfort? Weren't freedom from pain and the solace of caring and comforting attendants and family members, a death with dignity amid peaceful surroundings, the kind of care that were really wanted?

It took a British physician, Cicely Saunders, to found what became known as the modern hospice movement. Hospices had existed in Europe as early as the Middle Ages, where they served as havens or places of solace for wayfarers, religious pilgrims, and wounded soldiers. Later they evolved into lodgings for young people and travelers with limited means that were run by religious orders.

Dame Cicely Saunders, as she came to be titled, opened the first hospice for the dying, St. Christopher's, in London in 1967. Her goal was neither to speed up nor slow down the process of dying, but to provide the utmost possible in physical and emotional comfort to patients with a limited time left to live.

This meant not only the control of pain but of suffering resulting from feelings of abandonment. In an interview with the *Daily Telegraph* of London in 2002, Dame Cicely said, "I didn't set out to change the world. I set out to do something about pain. It wasn't long before I realized that pain wasn't only physical, but it was psychological and spiritual."

By the time Dame Cicely died in a London hospice in July 2005, at the age of eighty-seven, hundreds of hospices had been established in Great Britain and there were more than 3,000 in the United States, offering end-of-life care to nearly one million people a year. The first hospice in the United States was started in New Haven, Connecticut, in 1974.

Today most hospice care is home-based; that is, it serves patients who are in the final six months of their lives and who are visited, often daily, by physicians, nurses, medical technicians, social workers, counselors, and home aides. For persons who cannot be kept at home, there are residential hospices.

In either case, the goal is to provide what is known as palliative care. As defined by the World Health Organization (WHO), "Palliative care is the active total care of patients whose disease is not responsive to curative treatment. Control of pain, of other symptoms, and of psychological, social, and spiritual problems is paramount." In addition, it "offers a support system to help the family cope during the patient's illness and in their own bereavement."

The advent and expanding nature of hospice care should, in many cases, counteract the growing demands of the right-to-die movement. However, as hospice care is limited to patients diagnosed with six months or less to live, it may not serve the needs of those doomed to an unknown period of physical suffering, hopelessness, depression, loss of control, and anxiety about being a burden to others. Nor is hospice care available to patients who cannot express their wishes or feelings due to permanent unconsciousness, a persistent vegetative state, or irreversible brain damage.

THE RIGHT TO DIE and THE RIGHT TO LIFE

"The court's decision is based on the proposition, with which I agree, that life is precious and worthy of preservation without regard to its quality."

These were the words of Governor John Ashcroft of Missouri in March 1989, after the Missouri Supreme Court had denied Joe Cruzan, the parent and guardian of

Nancy Cruzan, the right to have his daughter's feeding tube removed so that her then six years in PVS might come to an end.

Governor Ashcroft, who would later become Attorney General of the United States during the first term of President George W. Bush, was one of a number of right-to-life advocates who—mainly for religious and/or political reasons—were opposed to all aspects of the right-to-die movement.

Principal among religious right-to-life groups are the Roman Catholic Church, fundamentalist Protestant sects such as Evangelical Christians, and Orthodox Jews. The National Right to Life Committee, which was formed in 1973 to oppose the pro-choice movement in the struggle to legalize abortion, has ties to the Catholic Church and supports the sanctity of life at the close of the human span as well as the beginning.

Political arguments against physician-assisted suicide are concerned with the danger that euthanasia, once approved by legislatures or courts, could be used too broadly. The old, the poor, and the neglected could be disposed of to save the cost and the responsibility of caring for them on the part of family members or public institutions.

The use of passive euthanasia, in the form of state-inflicted death in Nazi Germany, looms as a terrifying example. Between 1939 and 1941, the first two years of World War II in Europe, the government of Adolf Hitler murdered up to 100,000 German citizens who were deemed mentally or physically disabled. Their existence was seen as an economic and social burden on the fatherland in its pursuit of war and its conquest of other nations.

The medical profession has been and still is divided on the issue of assisted suicide. The traditional medical establishment adheres strictly to the Oath of Hippocrates, named for the fourth century BCE Greek physician and

Religious Right-to-Life Arguments

The principal argument of religious right-to-life groups, be they Catholic, Protestant, Jewish, or Muslim, is that all matters concerning death as well as birth are the domain of God. Life is seen as a gift from the creator, it is not to be controlled by humans, and suicide—whether assisted or self-administered—is as sinful as homicide.

The Roman Catholic view is expressed in *The Vatican Declaration on Euthanasia* of 1980. Among the points made are that intentionally causing one's own death is "a rejection of God's sovereignty and loving plan."

A statement by Pope John Paul II in 1995 does note that Roman Catholic teaching allows the dying to "forgo extraordinary or disproportionate" medical treatment but clearly cautions against suicide or euthanasia.

Some Protestant sects, such as the Christian Scientists, go so far as to put their complete faith regarding matters of health into the hands of God rather than that of physicians. As a result, they reject all forms of medical treatment, resorting exclusively to prayer as a cure for illness. Another Protestant offshoot, Jehovah's Witnesses, refuses blood transfusions.

While deaths among these religionists may, in some cases, be the direct result of refusal to seek vital medical help for one's self or for family members, they do not regard such deaths as suicides or homicides, but rather as an expression of the direct will of God.

As among traditional Catholics, certain Protestant groups, and Muslims and Orthodox Jews believe "the preservation of life" to be, in the words of Rabbi Yitzchok Breitowitz, "of paramount importance, surpassing virtually all of the other commandments of the Torah."

Human life, in fact, is so valuable that in order to preserve it or prolong it, Jews of the Orthodox persuasion may break the rules for fasting on the high holy day of Yom Kippur and even eat nonkosher food. In other words, Jewish law decrees that our bodies and our lives are not our own to do with as we will. Furthermore, the quality of the life being saved is irrelevant.

There is, however, a degree of flexibility even among Orthodox Jewry, allowing for refusal of aggressive medical treatment in terminal cases and accepting hospice care. So-called Conservative and Reform Jews tend to be even more accepting of certain right-to-die principles.

THOUGH DOCTORS REMAIN DIVIDED ON THE ISSUE OF ASSISTED SUICIDE, THOSE WHO HOLD SACRED THE TENETS OF THE HIPPOCRATIC OATH WOULD NOT AGREE THAT DOCTORS HAVE A RIGHT TO HELP PATIENTS DIE.

teacher who is credited with having written the vow that doctors still take today. One of the tenets of the Hippocratic Oath is "I will give no deadly medicine to anyone if asked, nor suggest any such counsel." This portion of the oath also states that the physician "will not give to a woman an instrument to produce abortion."

As a result, the American Medical Association (AMA), to which a large percentage of doctors belong, was slow to accept compulsory vaccinations for serious diseases and other public health innovations of the twentieth century. Nor was it until 1984 that it agreed to the withholding or withdrawing of life-sustaining treatment for patients who were permanently unconscious or dying if that was clearly the patient's wish.

Do we need a "right" to die? An overview of the first three quarters of the twentieth century indicates a growing conflict between two schools of thought.

As more Americans died in hospitals, where the terminally ill had their lives prolonged by the latest medical technologies, there was a growing demand for the right to control one's destiny through physician-assisted suicide, or voluntary euthanasia.

On the other hand, traditional religious, governmental, and medical philosophies were strongly opposed to such measures.

There remained a fundamental question that required consideration by both sides. If legally recognized, would PAS be safely limited only to those who clearly requested death with dignity, the so-called good death? Or, in the hands of the indifferent and the self-seeking, could the granting of PAS head down a slippery slope toward involuntary euthanasia, akin to the callous murders of the Hitler era?

For those right-to-life groups that saw the alleviation of terminal pain and suffering via PAS as too dangerous or too unprincipled to be undertaken, the alternative was to improve end-of-life care such as palliative treatment in a hospice situation.

But what about those patients who were not terminal, who still had long years of potential life ahead of them, and who were unable to express their wishes because they lived in the shadowy half-world of the comatose or the unconscious?

Karen Ann Quinlan, who first appeared on the scene in 1975, was one of those patients. She was twenty-one years old, she was being kept alive indefinitely on a respirator and a feeding tube, and she was in a persistent vegetative state. Her case, which would go on until 1985, made it clear that there were no simple answers to the right to die and the right to life.

Joseph and Julia Quinlan, the parents of Karen Ann Quinlan, look through a scrapbook of images of their daughter Karen before she was in a persistent vegetative state. As devout Catholics, the Quinlans turned to religious doctrine when they decided to ask to have their daughter's respirator turned off.

TWO
THE CASE OF KAREN ANN QUINLAN, 1975–1985

THE ONSET OF THE KAREN ANN QUINLAN CASE preceded that of Nancy Cruzan by eight years.

Both young women were victims of PVS, suffered similar symptoms of bodily disfiguration and medical deterioration, and were without hope of recovery.

Both had deeply caring parents and families that were keenly aware of their hopeless condition, and wanted to see it end. The element of religion, however, entered more strongly into the Quinlan case, which never went to the U.S. Supreme Court and was finally resolved by the New Jersey Supreme Court.

While the Cruzan case did go to the U.S. Supreme Court, it too was eventually resolved by a state court (in this case a trial court in Missouri), pointing to state legislatures and court systems as having historically played a broader role in dealing with right-to-die cases.

Karen Quinlan was a twenty-one-year-old New Jersey resident who lived at home with her parents and younger brother and sister as part of a devout Roman Catholic family. On the evening of April 15, 1975, Karen attended a party at which she consumed a combination of alcohol and drugs that caused her to stop breathing for not one but two periods of at least fifteen minutes each.

After friends at the party failed to revive her through mouth-to-mouth resuscitation, Karen was taken to a local hospital, Newton Memorial, where she was placed on a respirator to restore her breathing and where a tracheotomy (a surgical opening into the trachea, or airway, to the lungs) had been performed.

The restoration of Karen's breathing kept her alive, as did the introduction of a feeding tube, threaded through her nose to her stomach, for both nutrition and hydration. However, it was clear almost from the start of her hospitalization that she had suffered from anoxia, a lack of oxygen in her bloodstream for a prolonged period. As a result, she had sustained irreversible damage to the cortex of her brain.

Within a short time, Karen was removed to another hospital, St. Clare's in Denville, New Jersey, a Catholic institution, where she was placed under the care of Dr. Robert Morse. Numerous tests were performed. They included a brain scan and an electroencephalogram (EEG) to measure the electrical activity of the brain, as well as other neurological examinations.

The following information appeared in the 1976 case before the Supreme Court of New Jersey known as *In re Quinlan*, in the Matter of Quinlan (70 NJ 10). "Dr. Morse testified that Karen has been in a state of coma, lack of consciousness, since he began treating her. He explained that there are basically two types of coma, sleeplike unresponsiveness and awake unresponsiveness. Karen was originally in a sleeplike unresponsive condition but soon developed sleep-awake cycles, apparently a normal improvement for comatose patients within three to four weeks. In the awake cycle she blinks, cries out and does things of that sort but is still totally unaware of anyone or anything around her."

In addition to being in a chronic persistent vegetative

34

state, with no cognitive function, Karen had lost weight and her body had become shrunken and twisted. In the first six weeks she dropped from 115 to 90 pounds. Months later, even though feeding by tube continued, she had lost 40 pounds of her original weight and her body had become emaciated.

Typical of PVS patients was the way that Karen's body began to curl inward on itself soon after the injury to her brain: her elbows bent, forearms raised, and wrists pushed under her chin. Similarly, Karen's knees began to be drawn up toward her chest, so that she lay in a fetal position. Efforts to straighten her limbs by binding them to padded splints were of no avail.

Her daily care included monitoring her respirator and feeding, emptying her body wastes since normal urinary and bowel functions no longer took place, and suctioning mucus from her throat and nasal passages. Karen's temperature, pulse, and blood pressure had to be recorded every four hours. Every two hours she had to be turned to prevent bedsores. Nonetheless, the sores developed, especially at pressure points and where Karen's skin was so thin that her bones could be seen sticking through it.

THE QUINLAN FAMILY'S DECISION

The injury to Karen's brain had taken place in April 1975. The Quinlan family observed her dire mental and physical state, yet wondered if her life might go on as long as that of Elaine Esposito, the PVS patient who was still alive since having been stricken in 1941. (Esposito did not die until 1978.)

Was it possible that Karen would live to be nearly sixty without any cognitive response to the world around her, caged in a body that required constant care lest her bedsores multiply or her own bones bruise and cut her skin?

As a close-knit family that looked to its Catholic beliefs for direction, the Quinlans turned to their parish priest and longtime friend, Father Tom Trapasso. In view of the hopelessness of Karen's condition, was it possible that the Catholic Church would approve of a request from her family that her respirator be disconnected so that she could die a natural death if that was what God intended for her?

Father Trapasso consulted papal statements expressing Catholic doctrine on the use of "extraordinary" means to prolong lives with no hope of recovery, and he informed the Quinlans that he believed the removal of Karen's respirator was well within the Church's permissive boundaries.

Based on the findings of Father Trapasso with regard to Catholic doctrine in relation to Karen's condition, her family asked the hospital to remove her respirator and signed a release form to that effect. Initially, it appeared that the health care professionals at St. Clare's Hospital would cooperate. But within days, Dr. Robert Morse, the physician in charge of Karen's case, informed the Quinlans that he was morally opposed to the removal of her respirator, an act that would almost certainly cause her death and for which he refused to be responsible.

There was a further complication. Before becoming incompetent, Karen had executed no written directive as to how she wanted to live or die in the event of a serious illness or accident. In making a decision for her, Joseph Quinlan was attempting to act as her substitute, or surrogate. But since she was now over the age of twenty-one, he was no longer her legal guardian. In order to recommend the removal of the respirator, her father would have to go to court and have himself appointed her guardian.

The Quinlans were exploring new ground in their

FATHER TRAPASSO (R), THE QUINLANS' SPIRITUAL ADVISER, SHOWS THEM THE MASS HE WILL SAY IN HONOR OF THEIR DAUGHTER KAREN ON THE OCCASION OF HER FIRST BIRTHDAY WHILE IN A PERSISTENT VEGETATIVE STATE.

"EXTraorDinary" versus "orDinary" means

Father Trapasso's advice to the Quinlan family was based, firstly, on a declaration made as early as 1957 by Pope Pius XII to the effect that "Normally one is held to use only ordinary means," to preserve life. "That is to say, means that do not involve any grave burden for oneself or another. A more strict obligation would be too burdensome for most and would render the attainment of the higher, more important good too difficult."

The implication of the quote from Pope Pius XII appeared to be that keeping Karen alive on a respirator was an "extraordinary" or "disproportionate" measure. In other words, it offered no reasonable hope of benefiting the patient in terms of improving her condition or of easing her burden or that of her family.

By contrast, "ordinary" or "proportionate" means would be treatment that not only maintained the life of the patient but also held out some promise of improvement without being unduly burdensome.

A second source of religious permission for the removal of Karen's respirator appeared to come from *The Vatican Declaration on Euthanasia* of 1980. Although condemning suicide, whether self-inflicted or physician-assisted, this statement also held that patients were not obligated to undergo "extraordinary" or "disproportionate" medical treatment to preserve life. The judgment, however, as to the nature of a given means of treatment, was to be based on the personal, familial, economic, and social circumstances of the patient, as well as his or her religious beliefs.

IN 1975, THE QUINLANS ENLISTED THE ASSISTANCE OF LEGAL AID LAWYER PAUL W. ARMSTRONG IN THEIR FIGHT TO HAVE THEIR DAUGHTER'S RESPIRATOR REMOVED. ARMSTRONG FILED SUIT IN A NEW JERSEY CIVIL COURT, BUT HIS REQUEST WAS REJECTED.

effort to release their daughter from her vegetative mental state and the distortions and deterioration her body was undergoing. They had little acquaintance with the right-to-die movement as it had developed so far in the 1970s. All they had was their love for Karen, their family unity, their religious beliefs, and their conviction that the burden of their daughter's hopeless existence was too much for either her or them to carry.

With the help of a young Legal Aid attorney, Paul W. Armstrong, the Quinlans filed suit in a New Jersey civil court requesting that Joe Quinlan be named Karen's guardian and that her respirator be ordered to be removed.

Neither request was granted. A guardian who did not know Karen was appointed instead of her father, and the trial court judge, Robert Muir, declared, "There is no constitutional right to die that can be asserted by a parent for his incompetent adult child."

In his decision, rendered on November 10, 1975, Judge Muir added that physicians, not courts of law, were to be the arbiters of life-and-death decisions, and that the "morality and conscience of our society" belonged in the hands of the nation's doctors.

Who, however, was to decide which doctors were right and which were wrong? Was it acceptable for a doctor to keep alive a suffering patient without hope of recovery—whether competent or incompetent—as a result of personal religious beliefs, through fear of prosecution by the law, or just to feed that doctor's ego?

Shattered by Judge Muir's dismissal of the law's responsibility in Karen's case, the Quinlans immediately filed for an appeal and were gratified when the New Jersey Supreme Court—the highest in the state—bypassed the appeals court and agreed to hear the case.

THE VERDICT OF THE NEW JERSEY SUPREME COURT

By the time the *Quinlan* case was heard before the highest court in the state of New Jersey, almost a year had passed since the night of April 15, 1975. Karen's plight and the efforts of her family to put her into God's hands, as they saw it, had become a matter of national interest.

Both right-to-die and right-to-life factions made their feelings known. Reporters clustered around the

Quinlan house at all hours of the day and night, Karen's two younger siblings felt agitated and insecure, and legal as well as medical costs were making serious inroads on the Quinlans' finances.

Religious right-to-life groups that did not recognize the fine line between "extraordinary" and "ordinary" care, as defined by Catholic doctrine and as interpreted by the Quinlans and their parish clergy, sent the family hate mail and even threatened to "rescue" Karen from the removal of the respirator. As a result, a security guard had to be posted outside Karen's hospital room lest activist right-to-lifers attempted to take matters into their own hands.

Differing personal, medical, and religious opinions in the Quinlan matter might have festered indefinitely if not for the remarkably lucid and unanimous decision (7 to 0) rendered by Chief Justice Richard Hughes and the associate justices of the New Jersey Supreme Court.

On March 31, 1976, the Court declared that a "respirator or life support could be considered 'ordinary' in . . . the possibly curable patient but 'extraordinary' in the context of . . . an irreversibly doomed patient."

Much of the New Jersey Supreme Court's verdict thus rested on the issues of Karen's incurable condition as well as the right of the patient—or his or her surrogate—to refuse further treatment. Unlike the New Jersey civil court, which had appointed a stranger to be Karen's legal guardian, the state's supreme court determined that her father should fill the role of surrogate.

The right of Karen or, in this case, her surrogate to refuse life-prolonging treatment was based, in turn, on the right of privacy as it had been established by the U.S. Supreme Court in the 1973 abortion rights case known as *Roe* v. *Wade*.

While the word "privacy" does not appear anywhere in the U.S. Constitution or in its amendments, many judicial

karen quinlan's last years

The verdict of the New Jersey Supreme Court, with regard to the withdrawal of Karen's "present life-support system" in the interest of her right to privacy (as represented by her parent and guardian), would readily have permitted the removal of her feeding tube as well as her respirator. The Quinlan family, however, was of mixed opinions when it came to the possibility of denying Karen nutrition and hydration. Once again the question of employing "extraordinary" means to maintain the life of a comatose PVS patient came to the fore. But because there was disagreement within the family, the Quinlans did not request that the nursing home remove the feeding tube.

During Karen's final years her body continued to deteriorate. Dr. Robert Watson, the medical director of the Morris View Nursing Home stated that "She was so twisted that I couldn't even conceive the pain she would feel if she were to regain consciousness. One could only imagine the feeling if one would take a foot, twist it around a couple of times, and then tie it in that position, curled backward."

When Karen contracted pneumonia, the Quinlans once again rejected "extraordinary" means of trying to keep her alive, as in their decision to have her respirator removed. She was not given antibiotics and was allowed to die surrounded by members of her family.

The *Quinlan* case set three important legal precedents for the right-to-die issue. The right to privacy gave patients the right to refuse life-sustaining treatment, even in the face of death. Incompetent patients could have their patient's rights implemented through surrogates who were family members rather than the courts. And the state's interest in preserving life regardless of its quality could be overridden in cases where the treatment was excessive as related to the negative nature of the prognosis.

authorities have interpreted this right as being implicit in several amendments to the constitution.

The privacy right is seen to have its roots in such guarantees as freedom of religion, speech, press, and assembly (First Amendment). It reappears in the right of citizens to refuse to have soldiers billeted in their homes in time of peace (Third Amendment) and to be protected from unreasonable searches and seizures (Fourth Amendment). The Fifth and Fourteenth amendments include references to the protection of "life, liberty, or property" and the importance of "due process of law" and "equal protection of the laws" in preventing restriction or abuse of the guarantees of freedom and liberty.

So it is not surprising that in rejecting and overruling the lower court, the higher court wrote as follows: "Although the Constitution does not explicitly mention a right of privacy, [United States] Supreme Court decisions have recognized that a right of personal privacy exists and that certain rights of privacy are guaranteed under the Constitution."

The court, led by Chief Justice Hughes, analyzed Karen's situation as follows:

> The individual's right to privacy grows as the degree of bodily invasion increases and the prognosis dims. Ultimately there comes a point at which the individual's rights overcome the State interest. It is for this reason that we believe Karen's choice, if she were competent to make it, would be vindicated by the law. Her prognosis is extremely poor—she will never resume cognitive life. And the bodily invasion is very great—she requires 24 hour intensive nursing care, antibiotics, the assistance of a respirator, a catheter . . . and feeding tube.

In conclusion, the court granted Karen's surrogate, her father, the family's request stating that "the present life-support system may be withdrawn and said action shall be without any civil or criminal liability therefor on the part of any participant, whether guardian, physician, hospital, or others."

While the New Jersey Supreme Court had given permission for the imminent removal of Karen's respirator, weeks passed during which Dr. Robert Morse of St. Clare's Hospital failed to implement the court's decision. Finally, Morse told the Quinlans that both he and St. Clare's believed that such an act would be "morally incorrect." If the Quinlans wanted the respirator removed, Karen would have to be relocated to another facility.

On June 9, 1976, over two months after the court's decision, Karen was moved to the Morris View Nursing Home where, within a few days, she was taken off the respirator. To the surprise of her family and of the medical director of the new facility, Karen continued to breathe on her own.

The reasons for this unusual phenomenon were uncertain. Perhaps Karen's ability to survive without mechanical breathing assistance was due to her youth and general good health prior to her intake of alcohol and drugs on April 15, 1975. More likely, her survival had something to do with the fact that the staff at St. Clare's Hospital had started to wean her off the respirator after the court decision came down.

Was this an act of mercy or not? Continuing to be nourished by the feeding tube inserted into her stomach, Karen was kept alive for nine more years until her death from pneumonia on June 11, 1985.

THree
NANCY CRUZAN AND THE
MISSOURI STATE COURTS,
1983–1988

KAREN ANN QUINLAN WAS LIVING OUT the final two years of her life in a New Jersey nursing home at the time of the auto crash in Missouri that left another young woman, Nancy Beth Cruzan, in a similar persistent vegetative state.

In both cases (as well as those of some 14,000 other patients throughout the United States), the cause was permanent brain damage resulting from a short-term lack of oxygen. Between the time of Nancy's accident on January 11, 1983, and the day in October 1987 that the young lawyer, Bill Colby, met her for the first time, nearly five years had passed.

Nancy's parents had given more time to their hopes for her improvement or even recovery than had the family of Karen Ann Quinlan. In spite of the fact that Nancy had opened her eyes a week after the accident, she showed no response. As later described to Nancy's attorney, Bill Colby, "The skin on her face, still bruised and marked with stitches, had turned a sickly gray color and was dotted with acne spots. She had a seizure and somehow knocked a tooth out of the front of her mouth . . ."

Worst of all, Nancy's body and limbs began to exhibit the stiffening and curling upward and inward, known as contractures, that were typical of patients in the persistent vegetative state. CT scans and EEGs (electroencephalograms) had already shown that Nancy's cerebral cortex was dead and that the electrical activity in her brain was nearly, though not completely, flat. She had no bowel or bladder control, and had to be turned every two hours or so to prevent bedsores.

Nancy's only "improvement" was that she regained the ability to breathe without a respirator. However, a tracheotomy hole in her neck was left open for additional breathing and for suctioning mucus from her throat to prevent choking. The final step toward Nancy's long-term maintenance was taken in early February of 1983, when Nancy's father, Joe Cruzan, signed a consent form to have a feeding tube surgically inserted into her stomach.

Nancy could not take medicine, food, or liquids by mouth and she was not receiving enough nutrition, either intravenously or through a nasal feeding tube. Joe Cruzan did not know, however, that at the same time that he had given permission to have the feeding tube implanted, he had lost the right to have it removed.

One of the difficulties concerning the removal of a feeding tube, once implanted, had to do with the following. While a cognizant patient who had written a Living Will could request that a medical device such as a respirator be turned off, a feeding tube was not considered "medical" treatment according to Missouri state law. It was defined instead as a "procedure to provide nutrition and hydration."

In October 1987, when the family of Nancy Cruzan first appealed to the courts, their daughter had no legal access to a right to die. For one thing, even if Nancy had wanted to write a Living Will while she was still healthy, she could not have done so. Missouri's Living Will law did not go into effect until 1985, two years after Nancy's accident.

IN OCTOBER 1987, LAWYER WILLIAM COLBY AGREED TO TAKE NANCY BETH
CRUZAN'S CASE TO THE COURTS.

In addition, there was the question of Nancy's comatose state. What rights did a patient have if she was unable
to speak for herself? How could she voice her desires; how
could she exercise her right of privacy?

The First Missouri Court Decision

Nancy Cruzan's lawyer, Bill Colby, brought her case to
trial for the first time at the Jasper County Courthouse in
Carthage, Missouri, in March 1988. The specific purpose
of his suit was to have the presiding judge, Charles E. Teel,
request that the Missouri Rehabilitation Center—where
Nancy was now a long-term patient—should remove her
feeding tube. The decision was in the hands of Judge Teel
himself. There was no jury.

Colby's argument was based on Nancy's right to privacy and on the right of her parents, as her legal guardians, to speak for her. He also would try to establish that had Nancy been able to speak for herself she would not have wanted to live, possibly for thirty years or more, in a persistent vegetative state.

Right-to-life advocates might argue that the removal of a feeding tube was a criminal act similar to abortion. But Nancy was not a healthy fetus with all the possibilities of life open to her. She was a thirty-one-year-old woman irreversibly doomed to a limited form of existence that was entirely dependent on artificial feeding and on constant nursing and medical care.

In his presentation, Colby described Nancy's condition in detail, as well as the anguish of her family and their agreement in wanting to have the feeding tube removed. He also made a point of having the process of death in a PVS patient explained, based on the testimony of a medical expert.

"The testimony you will hear about her death," Colby told the judge, "will be that it is a peaceful one, that a person in a persistent vegetative state . . . is incapable of experiencing pain, incapable of experiencing thirst, incapable of experiencing hunger. . . . There is nothing left in their brain to experience these things. All they have left is brain stem function, which controls their reflexes."

The state of Missouri was represented at the trial by the assistant attorney general, Robert Presson, whose job it was to defend against the Cruzan plea. Presson's argument against the removal of the feeding tube was based on the principle that in making life-and-death decisions, it was better for the state to err on the side of life.

On the more specific issue of what Nancy would have wanted had she been able to voice her feelings, the assistant attorney general argued for "clear and convincing

NANCY CRUZAN'S CASE FIRST WENT TO TRIAL AT THE JASPER COUNTY
COURTHOUSE IN CARTHAGE, MISSOURI, IN MARCH 1988.

evidence" that Nancy would have preferred to die rather
than exist in her present condition.

Colby was uncomfortable with Presson's demand for
such evidence, for it would be difficult to obtain. Nancy
had never contemplated that at the age of twenty-five she
would be thrown more than thirty feet from her speeding
car, which had eventually come to a stop by flipping over
upside down. Nor, as far as he knew, had she ever envi-
sioned being in a vegetative state for the rest of her life.

During the three days that the trial before Judge Teel
lasted, a number of witnesses, chiefly medical doctors

who had treated Nancy over the years, were called to tes-
tify. The first neurologist who had seen Nancy soon after
the accident reviewed his original diagnosis of PVS and
his prognosis regarding her chances of recovery. They
were "nil." He also explained that in a patient without a
functioning brain, the withdrawal of the feeding tube
would create no perceptions of pain, hunger, or thirst.

Was it at all possible that once the feeding tube had
been removed Nancy would be able to resume taking suf-
ficient food and liquids in a normal manner, and therefore would not necessarily be condemned to starvation
and dehydration?

Neurologist and medical ethicist Dr. Ronald Cranford
testified that it was highly unlikely that a person who had
been in a vegetative state for as long as Nancy had would be
able to regain the ability to swallow without the danger of
aspirating (drawing) food into her lungs. In other words,
the act of swallowing "required consciousness and
thought, abilities a vegetative patient had lost forever.

"Many vegetative patients," Cranford admitted, "did
retain a primitive swallowing reflex, so food placed care-
fully on the tongue near the back of the throat could cause
the patient to 'swallow,' forcing the food down the esophagus to the stomach. An extremely careful and patient
nurse could possibly force enough into a PVS patient to
sustain the patient for a short time. But the staff at a
nursing home could never spend two to three hours per
meal on such primitive reflex feedings."

In addition, there was the ever-present danger that
food could be regurgitated from the stomach into the
esophagus and thence into the windpipe, bringing on a
case of pneumonia.

Cranford's testimony indicating that the feeding tube
was essentially a means of keeping Nancy alive led Bill
Colby to try to convince Judge Teel that a feeding tube was

IS a SURGICALLY INSERTED FEEDING TUBE a MEDICAL DEVICE?

In a further effort to classify a feeding tube as a medical device, Nancy's lawyer, Bill Colby, read into the court record a description of the process by which Nancy's tube had been inserted on February 7, 1983.

Colby described the operative procedure, derived word-for-word from Nancy's hospital record, as follows: "The abdominal area was prepped and draped. A previous upper midline incision was anesthetized with a 1 percent plain Xylocaine anesthesia, IV sedation, Pryor group. The incision was opened. Bleeders were electrocoagulated. The peritoneal cavity was entered."

Colby continued to read the medical description of the insertion of the feeding tube into the stomach itself, the tying of the purse string that secured the tube in place, and the manner in which the stomach was stitched to the underside of the peritoneum.

Finally, concluding with the bonding of the fascia (connective tissue) and the peritoneum, "skin and subcutaneous tissue were closed with skin clips. The patient was taken to the recovery room in a stable condition." The hospital report was signed by the presiding surgeon, R. L. Willcoxon, M.D.

Colby's point that a feeding tube was a medical (and even a surgical) device in the same sense that a respirator was a medical device was an attempt to show that the state of Missouri's ruling to the contrary was illogical. Would Judge Teel take this matter under consideration in issuing a verdict on the removal of Nancy Cruzan's feeding tube?

really a form of medical treatment. This position had already been taken by the American Medical Association, which regarded a feeding tube as medically necessary as a respirator.

However, the assistant attorney general, Bob Presson, representing the state of Missouri, pointed out that the AMA had also made the statement that "Life should be cherished despite disabilities and handicaps, except when the prolongation would be inhumane and unconscionable." Nancy, he ascertained upon questioning one of the doctors, was still a person, still a human being, and therefore one whose life, in the opinion of the state of Missouri, was to be cherished.

National interest in the trial in the small courthouse in Carthage, Missouri, had been growing ever since the Cruzan family announced its decision to request that Nancy's feeding tube be removed.

The court was still in session and the case was as yet undecided on the evening in March 1988 when Nancy's father, Joe Cruzan, and her sister Chris appeared on the nationally televised talk show *Nightline*, presided over by its well-known host and public affairs commentator, Ted Koppel.

Koppel opened the program with a description of Nancy's condition of the past five years and explained that she was:

> Unable in any manner to function on her own, with two very crucial exceptions: Her heart continues to pump blood through her body and she is breathing on her own. She could live, if that is the appropriate term, for many, many more years. Her family doesn't think she should. And so, they have petitioned a court—and here is where the case becomes so painfully complicated—to authorize

the removal of a feeding tube from the woman's stomach. Without nourishment, of course, she will eventually die.

The Koppel program included discussions with two doctors, one of them Ronald Cranford, who was appearing at the trial, and the other—also a medical ethicist—from the University of Chicago. The two were in agreement about Nancy's medical condition. She was just as unconscious as if she were brain-dead (the accepted medical criterion for death in the state of Missouri since 1982). But because of the reflex movements of her face and body, the fact that her heart was pumping and she was breathing on her own, she was alive. What could not easily be agreed upon were the ethical and moral principles of removing the feeding tube that sustained her.

Joe Cruzan, when it came his turn to speak on the program, expressed the anguish he and his family were undergoing at what they had already experienced as the loss of Nancy. "If the decision's wrong, if we're playing God, then I'll have to live with that, and I'm willing to."

The trial before Judge Teel in Carthage, Missouri, ended three days after it began, in March 1988. But it was not until July 27, 1988, that a ruling was delivered.

In the closing days of the trial, Bob Presson, the Missouri assistant attorney general, called to the witness stand nurses and other medical personnel from the Missouri Rehabilitation Center who saw Nancy on a daily basis. In direct contradiction of the capacities of a PVS patient, these witnesses testified that Nancy was responsive and even alert, that her eye movements, her grimaces, and her other facial expressions indicated that she could experience pain and pleasure, and that she knew what was going on around her.

Were these witnesses reading meaning into Nancy's

stares and throat sounds because daily attendance on an unresponsive patient is so numbing even to a professional caregiver? Or was there really a consciousness operating in Nancy's brain?

Other factors that delayed Judge Teel's decision were the *amicus curiae* briefs that were filed by groups both supporting and opposed to the right to die. *Amicus curiae,* which is Latin for "friend of the court," refers to the statements or arguments that interested parties ask to be read into the record of the court proceedings. Among right-to-life organizations involved were the Missouri Citizens for Life and the National Legal Center for the Medically Dependent and Disabled.

Anxiously the Cruzan family awaited word from the court. Losing the case meant more years for Nancy's wasted body and her family to endure. Winning the case meant a death sentence for Nancy. There was really no such thing as winning. For the Cruzans, Nancy had died five-and-a-half years ago. What they were asking for from the court was to permit their daughter the dignity of a bodily departure.

Judge Teel's ruling of July 27, 1988, turned out to have both a positive and a negative effect on the Cruzan case. Initially it looked like a "win" for the Cruzan family.

It read as follows:

There is a fundamental right expressed in our Constitution as the right to liberty which permits an individual to refuse or direct the withholding or withdrawal of artificial death prolonging procedures when the person has no more cognitive brain function than our Ward and all the physicians agree there is no hope of further recovery while the deterioration of the brain continues with further overall worsening physical contractures.

The Respondents, employees of the state of
Missouri, are directed to cause the request of the
Co-guardians to withdraw nutrition or hydration
to be carried out. Such a request having Court
approval, shall be taken the same as a request for
discontinuance of any other form of artificial life
support systems.

Judge Teel's directive to the Missouri Rehabilitation
Center was clear. The hospital was to disconnect Nancy
Cruzan's feeding tube and to allow the natural conse-
quences of its removal to take place.

The court order that the Cruzans had been waiting for,
however, was not to be carried out. Not only did the hospital refuse to follow it, but within days, the state of
Missouri appealed Judge Teel's decision and called for a
higher court to review it.

The Missouri Supreme Court, the highest court in the
state, would hear the appeal. Once more, Nancy's status
was in question and once more the Cruzan family had to
put its hopes for a resolution to this painful matter on hold.

THE second missouri court decision

The Missouri Supreme Court heard the Cruzan case in
September 1988, in Jefferson City, the Missouri state capital. Again there was no jury. This court was composed of
seven judges, who would render a majority opinion. In
that regard, the Missouri Supreme Court operated similarly to the U.S. Supreme Court, except that the latter con-
sisted of nine justices.

In revisiting the case, Colby made extensive notes in
an effort to leave no stone unturned in pleading Nancy's
cause. He argued for the individual rights of privacy and
liberty under the Constitution. He pointed out that six
doctors, three of whom were on staff at the Missouri

Rehabilitation Center, had confirmed the diagnosis of Nancy's condition as PVS and therefore irreversible.

Colby tried to convince the judges that Nancy's feeding tube was a form of medical treatment and therefore its surgical implantation had been an invasion of her body without her consent. Nor had the feeding tube served as a means of recovery as originally intended. And he made every attempt to convince the court that Nancy's family, as those who knew her longest and best, should be given the right to speak for her.

Bob Presson, the assistant attorney general, again speaking for the state, urged the Missouri Supreme Court to overturn the lower court's decision, which had been characterized by right-to-life groups as akin to homicide, as carried out by starvation.

The length of the second Missouri trial was extended through the addition of *amicus curiae* briefs from many more groups, both in support of and in opposition to the Cruzan case. When the court's decision was finally delivered on November 16, 1988, the verdict was 4 to 3 against the Cruzans.

The majority opinion stated that Missouri law did not provide Nancy's parents with the right to choose her death, and that it was entirely possible that incompetent patients might choose to live in spite of their diminished quality of life. In short, the state of Missouri stood by the principle that it was preferable to make an error on the side of life rather than to uphold the decision of the lower court that Nancy's feeding tube should be removed.

The three judges who had dissented from the majority on the Missouri Supreme Court made sympathetic statements, upholding the courage of Judge Teel's decision. One of the dissenters, Judge Blackmar, stated with regard to Nancy, "If she has any awareness of her surroundings, her life must be a living hell."

Pro-life groups, on the other hand, praised the decision of the Missouri Supreme Court. The legislative chairman of Missouri Citizens for Life stated, "It's reassuring that the Missouri courts agree that handicapped patients have the same right to receive the basic care, including food and water, that is provided to the non-handicapped."

In any case, the majority opinion of the second Missouri court stood, and the question for Bill Colby and the Cruzans was what to do next. Colby was not ready to give up. There were three options, although admittedly farfetched, that still remained. One was to petition the Missouri Supreme Court for a re-hearing of the case.

The second option was to give up on Missouri entirely and move Nancy to another state, where the patient's right of privacy and the insights of her parental surrogates might count for more than the impersonal rulings of the state government. New Jersey, where Karen Quinlan's case had been tried in the highest court, had proved an example.

The third option was to try to have Nancy's case heard by the highest court in the land, the U. S. Supreme Court. Chances, however, that the Supreme Court would accept the Cruzan case appeared slim. Of the thousands of cases that the Court was asked to take each year, only a couple of hundred were accepted.

The acceptance of a case is known as *certiorari*, an agreement by a superior court to call up the records of a lower, or inferior, court. For a *writ of certiorari* to be issued, four of the nine Supreme Court justices must vote in favor. In view of the enormous range and number of such petitions that the Court received, would the Cruzans stand a chance of having Nancy's case reviewed by the nine justices that included some of the most distinguished legal minds in the United States?

four
NANCY CRUZAN AND THE
SUPREME COURT, 1989–1990

DURING THE SUMMER OF 1989, discussion of the
Nancy Cruzan case was uppermost in the national media.
The U.S. Supreme Court had agreed to take the first right-
to-die case in its two-hundred-year history. A slim
margin of four justices had voted in favor of hearing
Cruzan v. *Director, Missouri Department of Health*, while the
remaining five had opposed it.

It was felt that *Cruzan* v. *Missouri*, as it came to be popularly known, was certain to be a landmark case. It was
hoped that in hearing arguments from both the Cruzans
and the state of Missouri the Court would hand down a
definitive judgment regarding the right of terminally or
irreversibly ill patients to refuse life-prolonging medical
treatment.

It was also hoped that in the case of incompetent
patients, such as Nancy and about 14,000 others all over
the country, the question of the right of parents or other
surrogates to make life-and-death decisions would be
resolved.

Appearing on national television on *Good Morning
America* in August 1989, Nancy's parents, Joe and Joyce
Cruzan, stated, as they had on several broadcasts and tele-
casts in the past, that since her accident Nancy had never

shown any responses to stimuli or made any signs of recognition. They accepted the decision of the doctors that her condition was irreversible. Yet, with the feeding tube, she could live in a steadily worsening physical condition for another thirty or forty years.

The Cruzans were already familiar with the opposition that they faced from the state government of Missouri. In March 1989, following the Missouri Supreme Court's verdict, Governor John Ashcroft had informed Joe Cruzan by letter that he believed life to be "worthy of preservation without regard to its quality" and added, "I am not at ease with the notion that the legislature can empower anyone, no matter how close to the person, to decide to make that person die by withholding food and water."

Public opinion was also being influenced by the words of the Christian evangelist religious leader Pat Robertson when he told the members of his 700 Club in the summer of 1989, "Euthanasia, the right to die, or the right to kill? [Nancy Cruzan] can experience pain and joy: she expresses tears and smiles. But she was sentenced to die a horrible and painful death by starvation."

Now, on *Good Morning America*, a Missouri state senator, John Schneider, brought up the fact that nurses had testified that Nancy *did* follow voices with her eyes and respond to pain stimuli. In denying her and patients like her food and water, Missouri might well be venturing down a slippery slope toward killing hundreds of people in nursing homes all over the state who simply had a poor quality of life.

The final guest on the show was Harvard Law professor Arthur Miller. Did the fact that the Supreme Court had taken the Cruzan case, while having refused the Quinlan case of some years earlier, mean that major changes were on the horizon? Miller agreed that the right to refuse medical treatment, especially in the face of

CHRISTIAN COALITION FOUNDER PAT ROBERTSON LED THE FIGHT AGAINST THE RIGHT OF NANCY CRUZAN TO BE TAKEN OFF ARTIFICIAL LIFE SUPPORT.

irreversible or terminal illness, was a growing issue. But he warned his television hosts, as well as the Cruzans, not to expect too much in the way of sweeping announcements from the Court.

Was he right or wrong? The hearing before the U.S. Supreme Court was to take place on December 6, 1989. Bill Colby, the Cruzans' lawyer, would be arguing his first case before that august body. It could well be months before the opinion of the Court was rendered. Only time would tell.

THE SUPREME COURT EXAMINES AND RULES ON *CRUZAN* V. *MISSOURI*

The Cruzan family and also the family of William Colby, Nancy's lawyer, were present in the courtroom on the day that they and the entire nation had long awaited. The Supreme Court had taken its first case concerning what was commonly referred to as the right to die. Would the Court find that the U.S. Constitution granted personal liberties with regard to that right, which could not be overruled by the state of Missouri?

Shortly after ten o'clock on the morning of December 6, Chief Justice William Rehnquist called Colby to the podium to argue his case. A lengthy explanation of Nancy's illness and its background was not required. The justices had studied the briefs in advance and knew that the lawyer for the plaintiff was asking for her feeding tube to be disconnected in order to allow her to die.

Remarks and queries from the justices came thick and fast. Justice Antonin Scalia plunged right in with the question as to whether Nancy could be "fed manually by . . . massaging the food down her throat or something of that sort. Is that correct or not?"

Colby replied that Nancy was presently incapable of receiving nourishment in that way, and was forced to

A Hearing Day at the Supreme Court

The U.S. Supreme Court building in Washington, D.C., is a glittering, white marble edifice, impressive in its majesty and austerity. It was constructed in 1935. In earlier incarnations, this highest court in the nation's judicial system existed in more modest quarters, starting in 1790 in New York City and moving to Washington in 1800, when that city became the nation's capital.

Throughout its history, however, the rules of the Court have remained essentially the same. Its decisions on cases that affect the entire country are final. Most, but not all, of its cases are appeals from either state courts or lesser federal courts. The remainder may be cases that deal with disputes between the states or between a state and the federal government. Slavery, school segregation, and abortion have been among some of the major issues the Court has decided during its more than two hundred years of numerous and varied deliberations. These are known as landmark decisions.

The Court's term—the period during which it hears cases—runs from the first Monday in October to about the end of June. Decisions may be rendered at any time during the hearing term or at the close of it. Not every day during the term is a hearing day. There may be two weeks of hearing cases and then two weeks of recess to review them.

A hearing day begins at 10 AM with the robed justices sitting at a long mahogany table, known as the bench. Soaring marble columns and rich maroon curtains frame the background. The Court's chief justice sits in the middle of the dais, the other justices arrayed on either side—in descending order—according to the length of time they have served on the Court.

Lawyers on both sides of the issue, who have already presented their written briefs detailing all the facts in the case, submit oral arguments, each lawyer taking his or her turn to speak from a stand facing the justices. There are no witnesses called and, of course, no jury.

The justices take turns questioning each of the opposing lawyers on the case, with only thirty minutes allowed per presentation. Very few members of the general public are able to secure seats for the day's hearing and those who do may not leave the courtroom during the session for which they have seats. The morning session runs from 10:00 AM to noon and the afternoon from 1:00 PM to 3:00 PM, Tourists who merely want a glimpse of the Court in session are permitted to cycle through the back of the courtroom at brief intervals during which they must keep moving.

It is a moment of both rigid formality and high excitement when, at the start of a hearing day, the marshal of the Court is heard to cry out, "The Honorable, the Chief Justice, and the Associate Justices of the Supreme Court of the United States. Oyez! Oyez! Oyez! All persons having business before the Honorable, the Supreme Court of the United States, are admonished to draw near and give their attention, for the Court is now sitting. God save the United States and this Honorable Court."

The justices, usually the full complement of nine, now emerge from behind the maroon curtains and take their seats at the bench. The day's hearing is about to begin.

admit that the Cruzan family had given its consent for the surgical insertion of the feeding tube that it now wanted to have withdrawn.

Justice Sandra Day O'Connor, the first woman to be appointed to the Court (in 1981), wanted to know if a competent adult had the right to refuse food and water in a hospital setting. Wouldn't that be considered irrational and wouldn't the state have the right to interfere on the side of life?

Other justices entered the discussion, which centered briefly on whether a patient, competent or not, had the right to commit suicide. As Colby's time was beginning to run out, so that the attorneys for the state of Missouri could come to the stand, he made a final plea for Nancy's right to liberty under the Fourteenth Amendment of the Constitution.

Although the Fourteenth Amendment, ratified in 1868, was passed to protect the citizenship rights of the newly freed slaves after the Civil War, it is a document that lends itself to broad interpretation with regard to the rights and legal protection of all citizens.

In part, the Fourteenth Amendment reads: "No State shall make or enforce any law which shall abridge the privileges or immunities of citizens of the United States; nor shall any State deprive any person of life, liberty, or property, without due process of law; nor deny any person within its jurisdiction the equal protection of the law."

In concluding, Colby argued that the state of Missouri had been in violation of the "liberty" right of the Fourteenth Amendment because it had interfered with Nancy's privacy, denying her the opportunity to die with dignity and condemning her to untold years of ongoing decline and hopelessness.

Oral arguments before the Court continued with Robert Presson, the assistant attorney general of Missouri,

THE SUPREME COURT AT THE TIME OF THE CRUZAN CASE: FRONT (LEFT TO RIGHT): ASSOCIATE JUSTICES THURGOOD MARSHALL AND WILLIAM BRENNAN, CHIEF JUSTICE WILLIAM REHNQUIST, ASSOCIATE JUSTICES BYRON WHITE AND HARRY BLACKMUN. REAR (LEFT TO RIGHT): ASSOCIATE JUSTICES ANTONIN SCALIA, JOHN PAUL STEVENS, SANDRA DAY O'CONNOR, AND ANTHONY KENNEDY.

arguing for the decision of the Missouri Supreme Court to stand, on the ground that it had been correct in denying Nancy's parents' request to have her feeding tube removed.

Presson, who was accompanied by the Missouri

THrouGH THe court system

First Stop: State Court
Almost all cases (about 95 percent) start in state courts.
These courts go by various names, depending on the state
in which they operate: circuit, district, municipal, county,
or superior. The case is tried and decided by a judge, a
panel of judges, or a jury.
The side that loses can then appeal to the next level.

First Stop: Federal Court
U.S. DISTRICT COURT—About 5 percent of cases begin
their journey in federal court. Most of these cases concern
federal laws, the U.S. Constitution, or disputes that
involve two or more states. They are heard in one of the
ninety-four U.S. district courts in the nation.
U.S. COURT OF INTERNATIONAL TRADE—Federal court
cases involving international trade appear in the U.S.
Court of International Trade.
U.S. CLAIMS COURT—The U.S. Claims Court hears federal cases that involve more than $10,000, Indian claims,
and some disputes with government contractors.
The loser in federal court can appeal to the next level.

Appeals: State Cases
Forty states have appeals courts that hear cases that have
come from the state courts. In states without an appeals
court, the case goes directly to the state supreme court.

Appeals: Federal Cases
U.S. CIRCUIT COURT—Cases appealed from U.S. district
courts go to U.S. circuit courts of appeals. There are twelve
circuit courts that handle cases from throughout the

nation. Each district court and every state and territory are assigned to one of the twelve circuits. Appeals in a few state cases—those that deal with rights guaranteed by the U.S. Constitution—are also heard in this court.

U.S. COURT OF APPEALS—Cases appealed from the U.S. Court of International Trade and the U.S. Claims Court are heard by the U.S. Court of Appeals for the Federal Circuit. Among the cases heard in this court are those involving patents and minor claims against the federal government.

Further Appeals: State Supreme Court

Cases appealed from state appeals courts go to the highest courts in the state—usually called supreme court. In New York, the state's highest court is called the court of appeals. Most state cases do not go beyond this point.

Final Appeals: U.S. Supreme Court

The U.S. Supreme Court is the highest court in the country. Its decision on a case is the final word. The Court decides issues that can affect every person in the nation. It has decided cases on slavery, abortion, school segregation, and many other important issues.

The Court selects the cases it will hear—usually around one hundred each year. Four of the nine justices must vote to consider a case in order for it to be heard. Almost all cases have been appealed from the lower courts (either state or federal).

Most people seeking a decision from the Court submit a petition for certiorari. Certiorari means that the case will be moved from a lower court to a higher court for review. The Court receives about nine thousand of these requests annually. The petition outlines the case and gives reasons why the Court should review it.

In rare cases, for example *New York Times* v. *United States*, an issue must be decided immediately. When such a case is of national importance, the Court allows it to bypass the usual lower court system and hears the case directly.

To win a spot on the Court's docket, a case must fall within one of the following categories:

- Disputes between states and the federal government or between two or more states. The Court also reviews cases involving ambassadors, consuls, and foreign ministers.

- Appeals from state courts that have ruled on a federal question.

- Appeals from federal appeals courts (about two-thirds of all requests fall into this category).

attorney general, William Webster, made the point before the justices that there was no undue financial burden on the Cruzan family. The state of Missouri was paying for Nancy's care in the Missouri Rehabilitation Center and no time limit on her stay had been set. She could, in other words, remain there indefinitely.

As in the first two court trials held in Missouri, the Supreme Court hearing drew a number of *amicus curiae* briefs. About fifty organized groups that had an interest in the case filed such "friend of the court" entries, either supporting the Cruzans or agreeing with the position of the state of Missouri.

Also, as George H. W. Bush, then president of the United States, took an interest in the Cruzan case, he had the federal government's chief legal officer at the time, Solicitor General Kenneth Starr, file a statement. Starr's oral argument agreed with that of Robert Presson. It favored the stand taken by the state of Missouri.

Starr's view was that it was up to the individual states to make decisions on right-to-die matters. He added that a feeding tube was not essentially a medical device and that a health care facility should not be forced by a court to withdraw nutrition and hydration in the case of an incompetent person.

The hearing of the case known as *Cruzan, by her Parents and Co-Guardians* v. *Director, Missouri Department of Health*, Supreme Court of the United States, 497 U.S. 261, had taken approximately one hour for the lawyers to present their arguments and answer the questions of the nine justices. Each side had been given its allotted half hour, ending with a yellow warning light and a red stop light. Now there was nothing left to do but wait for the decision of the highest court in the land.

The months following the December 6, 1989, hearing dragged by. They were an anxious time for the Cruzans and a period of intense discussion in the media on both sides of the issue. Finally, on June 25, 1990, after sixth months, the Court announced its decision.

By a vote of 5 to 4, the Cruzan plea for a right to die for Nancy was denied.

Chief Justice Rehnquist wrote the majority opinion. Justices Antonin Scalia, Sandra Day O'Connor, Byron R. White, and Anthony M. Kennedy joined the Chief Justice in his summation, which upheld the judgment of the Supreme Court of Missouri.

In other words, while the Supreme Court recognized the right of competent individuals to refuse medical treatment, it did not recognize the right of family members of incompetent patients to request that life-support systems be disconnected and that the patient should be allowed to die. In Nancy's case, according to Justice Rehnquist, the state of Missouri had been correct in its demand for "clear and convincing evidence" of Nancy's desire to die and its refusal to accept "substituted judgment."

"In sum," Justice Rehnquist wrote, "we conclude that a State may apply a clear and convincing standard in proceedings where a guardian seeks to discontinue nutrition and hydration of a person diagnosed to be in a persistent vegetative state. . . .We cannot say that the Supreme Court of Missouri committed constitutional error in reaching the conclusion that it did."

Justice Scalia, who was in agreement with Justice Rehnquist, wrote a concurring opinion that went even further, asserting his belief that the states rather than the federal government have jurisdiction over the right to die.

"While I agree with the Court's analysis today, and therefore join in its opinion, I would have preferred that we announce, clearly and promptly, that the federal courts have no business in this field; that American law has always accorded the State the power to prevent, by force if

JUSTICE WILLIAM J. BRENNAN JR. WROTE THE DISSENTING OPINION IN THE
CRUZAN CASE, CITING PRIVACY CONCERNS TO WHICH HE BELIEVED NANCY
CRUZAN WAS ENTITLED.

necessary, suicide—including suicide by refusing to take appropriate measures necessary to preserve one's life."

The four dissenting justices were William Brennan, Harry Blackmun, John Paul Stevens, and Thurgood Marshall.

Justice Brennan, with whom Justices Blackmun and Marshall agreed, wrote a dissenting opinion in defense of the privacy concerns that he felt should have been granted to Nancy Cruzan by the Court.

"Medical technology has effectively created a twilight zone of suspended animation where death commences while life, in some form, continues. Some patients, however, want no part of a life sustained by medical technology. Instead, they prefer a plan of medical treatment that allows nature to take its course and permits them to die with dignity."

Justice Brennan went on to write, "Nancy Cruzan has dwelt in that twilight zone for six years." He referred to the unconscious, reflexive twitches of her body, the ongoing degeneration of her brain, and the irreversible nature of her condition. "Because I believe that Nancy Cruzan has a fundamental right to be free of unwanted artificial nutrition and hydration, which right is not outweighed by any interests of the State, and because I find that the improperly biased procedural obstacles imposed by the Missouri Supreme Court impermissibly burden that right, I respectfully dissent."

The Brennan dissent closed with a warning. "The greatest dangers to liberty lurk in insidious encroachment by men of zeal, well meaning but without understanding."

Justice John Paul Stevens wrote his own dissenting opinion. He argued that "the State's abstract, undifferentiated interest in the preservation of life" was not in the "best interests of Nancy Beth Cruzan." Justice Stevens agreed with Nancy's lawyer, William Colby, regarding her "liberty" right under the Fourteenth Amendment. And he went on to quote liberally from the opinions of the three dissenting judges in the Missouri Supreme Court trial.

Justice Stevens concluded with the following statement, "The Cruzan family's continuing concern provides a concrete reminder that Nancy Cruzan's interests did not disappear with her vitality or her consciousness. However commendable may be the State's interest in human life, it cannot pursue that interest by appropriating Nancy Cruzan's life as a symbol for its own purposes."

The dissenting opinions of the four justices who had a more open view of the interpretation of the Constitution and who took a more individualistic stance toward the Cruzans' request was heartening to Nancy's family. But it was not the majority opinion of the Court.

Yet it was in a careful rereading of the majority opinion, as written by Chief Justice Rehnquist, that Colby caught a sudden glimpse of a new avenue to explore. As part of his opinion, Justice Rehnquist had written that "the possibility of subsequent developments such as . . . the discovery of new evidence regarding the patient's intent" might "at least create the potential that a wrong decision will eventually be corrected or its impact mitigated."

In other words, although the U.S. Supreme Court had denied the Cruzans the right to speak for Nancy, new evidence of her own wish to terminate a life in a persistent vegetative state might still allow a court to authorize the withdrawal of the feeding tube. Vague reports of conversations Nancy had had with friends prior to her accident had been drifting onto the scene as early as the first Missouri trial in Judge Teel's courtroom.

But the "clear and convincing evidence" that had been sought was not forthcoming because adequate witnesses to specific conversations with Nancy (stating that she

would not have wanted to be kept alive in a hopeless condition) could not be found.

The hearing of the case of *Cruzan* v. *Missouri* before
the Supreme Court changed all that. It had created broad
public awareness of Nancy's situation. A photograph of
her before the accident appeared on television and in the
newspapers. And her picture alerted former coworkers to
the fact that they had once known her. When they knew
her, however, Nancy Cruzan had been married to her
first, and later, to her second, husband. As a result, her
former friends had known her as either Nancy Hayes or
Nancy Davis.

Two substantial witnesses came forward. They were
young women who Nancy had worked with in the late
1970s at a small school for severely handicapped children
in Joplin, Missouri. Their names were Debi Havner (at
that time Debi Aaron) and Marianne Smith, and what they
had to report about conversations they had had with
Nancy was deeply indicative of her views on the futility of
living a life of severe mental and physical deprivation.

Colby saw the possibility of calling for a new trial for
Nancy in the court of Judge Teel, who had formerly been
sympathetic. Would the testimony of Debi Havner and
Marianne Smith finally provide the "clear and convincing
evidence" that the state of Missouri demanded for the
removal of Nancy's feeding tube?

THE FOURTH AND FINAL TRIAL

On November 1, 1990, a final trial began in the courtroom
of Judge Charles Teel in Jasper County, Missouri. It was
the second of Nancy's four trials to be held there. In addition to the new evidence that Colby was about to present,
Teel requested an update on Nancy's condition since her
case had first been tried in his court in March 1988.

The chief of neurosurgery at the University of

Missouri, Dr. Clark Watts, undertook Nancy's examination at the Missouri Rehabilitation Center. As in the past, Nancy lacked the ability to respond to requests from the doctor that she stick out her tongue, open her eyes, squeeze his hand. She did blink slightly when Dr. Watts clapped his hands sharply beside her ear. But the blinking was a reflex action, not a response to a question or a command.

The trial got under way with Colby calling first Marianne Smith to the stand and then Debi Havner. Both women attested to the conversations they had had with Nancy on the subject of the severely handicapped children under their care, and to Nancy's negative reaction to living as a "vegetable" and being force-fed.

When Colby asked Marianne Smith, "Do you have any doubt, in your mind, that Nancy would reject medical treatment being forced on her?" Smith replied, "No doubt."

Havner, who now lived in Arkansas and had given her written testimony under oath ten days earlier, agreed to fly to Carthage, Missouri, so that she could appear in person at the trial in the hope that it would be of additional benefit to Nancy.

The trial closed with testimony from Dr. James Davis, who had been seeing Nancy daily for three years. As her primary-care physician, Davis had originally disagreed with the removal of Nancy's feeding tube. Now he testified that he had changed his mind. Nancy's condition was hopeless. In response to questions from Colby as to Nancy's quality of life, Davis responded, "I think it would be personally a living hell."

On Friday, December 14, 1990, Judge Teel rendered his decision. There was now "clear and convincing evidence" that the choice of Nancy Cruzan, "if mentally able, would be to terminate her nutrition and hydration." The state of Missouri had withdrawn from the case, and so the

"CLear and convincing EVIDence"

It was early in 1978 when Debi Havner, who was a certified teacher of the hearing-impaired at the special school in Joplin, Missouri, hired Nancy Cruzan Hayes and Marianne Smith to work with her as teacher's aides. For six months, the three women were engaged in caring for four children ranging in age from three to preteen. All of the children were deaf, blind, and severely retarded. One wore leg braces and another was confined to a wheelchair. One of the four lived in a foster home and another in an institution. These children had been abused, and even the two who lived at home suffered from neglect.

There was little the teacher and her aides could do for their daily charges other than keep them clean and see to it that they were fed at school. Nancy took special care of three-year-old Melissa, who was wheelchair-bound and had to be fed with a small spoon and a syringe called an "InfaFeeder." The tiny, undersized child was beyond communication, and often rejected feeding with her tongue, so that food splattered over Nancy as well as Melissa.

Sitting in the classroom, the three women often discussed the dire condition of the children and their almost complete inability to experience the world around them. Nancy was especially upset about the force-feeding device she had to use to try to get nourishment into Melissa. All three women agreed, according to what Debi told Colby, that "we would never want to be tube-fed like that or fed with a feeder."

For want of a better word, Nancy had described Melissa as a "vegetable." Nancy didn't mean to be insensitive, but it was the only word she could think of for a life form with almost no human responsiveness.

Little did Nancy know at the time that the condition she was describing was eerily similar to the one she would encounter as a victim of the persistent vegetative state.

order to the Missouri Rehabilitation Center was to remove Nancy's feeding tube without delay.

Right-to-life groups had long been priming themselves to protest Judge Teel's decision if it should favor the Cruzans' request. Similarly, hospital personnel had a petition ready to sign, opposing the termination of Nancy's life. Nevertheless, at 3:20 PM on the afternoon of December 14, Davis removed Nancy's feeding tube, as ordered by the court.

Doctors estimated that it would take from ten days to two weeks for Nancy to die. Dr. Davis and others had offered repeated assurances that Nancy was incapable of feeling pain or thirst, or having any emotional response to the withdrawal of nutrition and hydration. Yet, over the days that followed, the protest groups that camped outside the hospital made efforts to find Nancy's room and bring her water.

Missouri's Governor Ashcroft received a request from Missouri Citizens for Life to order that Nancy's feeding tube be reinserted. But the governor was forced to admit that he had no authority in what was a state judicial matter. Therefore he was not eligible to act on the court's decision.

To make Nancy's death easier for the nurses and other staff members responsible for her personal care over the years, she was moved to another wing of the Missouri Rehabilitation Center. Her family visited her there every day until December 26, 1990, when she took her final breath.

Nearly eight years had passed between the night of Nancy's accident and her release from the persistent vegetative state that followed. The Cruzans felt that Nancy had died, however, on the night of her accident, January 11, 1983. Therefore her tombstone in the cemetery in Carterville, Missouri, her place of birth, reads:

Dr. James Davis, Nancy Cruzan's primary-care physician, originally opposed the removal of her feeding tube. By the time of the fourth and final trial in the Cruzan case, he had changed his mind, and testified that she should be allowed to die peacefully.

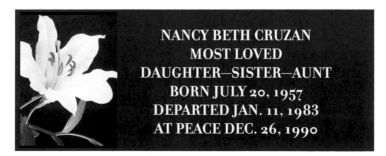

NANCY BETH CRUZAN
MOST LOVED
DAUGHTER—SISTER—AUNT
BORN JULY 20, 1957
DEPARTED JAN. 11, 1983
AT PEACE DEC. 26, 1990

THE AFTERMATH

Probably the most significant result of the Cruzan case was the authority it gave to competent individuals, as a result of the U.S. Supreme Court decision, to refuse medical treatment.

An immediate result was the Patient Self-Determination Act, which was introduced into Congress by Missouri's Republican Senator John Danforth. The bill passed in November 1990 and was signed into law on December 1, 1991.

The federal government, through this act, states that "medical facilities, including hospitals, nursing homes, home health organizations, and hospices receiving federal funds . . . must inform patients upon admission of the existence of state laws . . . regarding patients' rights."

On the other hand, in the case of incompetent individuals, such as Nancy Cruzan, the Supreme Court decision upheld the right of the individual states to demand "clear and convincing evidence" from families or other surrogates requesting that the irreversibly or terminally ill incompetent patient be allowed to refuse life support.

As a result of the Cruzan case, the Court did agree that a feeding tube was a form of medical treatment. But, once again, for incompetent patients, the individual would have had to leave clear instructions refusing a feeding tube.

How were such instructions to be left? The obvious answer is through the writing of a Living Will, a Health Care Proxy, or similar document, as previously discussed. Today, all states and the District of Columbia have laws regarding the use of advance directives that are recognized within their jurisdictions.

Copies of such documents should be within access of family members and should be provided to family doctors and to health care facilities upon admission. Unfortunately, however, severe and incapacitating illnesses are something that none of us like to contemplate.

As a result, today, many years after *Cruzan* v. *Missouri*—the first Supreme Court case dealing with the right to die—only about 20 percent of Americans have signed advance directives concerning their wishes in the event of serious illnesses, disabilities, or end-of-life problems.

Other than the federal directive—via the Patient Self-Determination Act of 1991, ordering that competent patients must be informed of their right to refuse medical treatment—there is nothing in the Constitution that protects a universal "right" to die.

Throughout the nation, state courts appear to prevail in cases regarding incompetent patients who have left no prior treatment instructions. And, as seen in the contrast between the Karen Quinlan case in the state of New Jersey and the Nancy Cruzan case in Missouri, these courts have varied in their approach to the removal of life-support systems.

Another difference among the states is that, while all are required to recognize a competent patient's right to refuse medical treatment, at this time only one state, Oregon, permits competent patients to request a more active means of ending their lives—that of assisted suicide.

Following *Cruzan* v. *Missouri*, the 1990s were a decade during which the issue of physician-assisted suicide became prominent. Was it enough to give a patient the right to refuse medication and life-support systems? What if the patient was suffering from a painful disabling illness that made life unbearable despite the best medical efforts to ease the patient's physical misery and emotional anguish?

In 1990, the public's attention was drawn to the work of Dr. Jack Kevorkian who, by the time he was convicted of physician-assisted suicide (PAS) in 1999, had provided more than a hundred patients with the means to end their lives.

In 1994 the state of Oregon voted to approve a Death with Dignity Act permitting terminally ill patients who could meet a certain set of conditions to obtain from their doctor a medical prescription that would bring about their death.

And in 1997, the U.S. Supreme Court agreed to hear two cases on the subject of PAS. The questions that would come into play, then or later, were: "Does a person have a constitutional right to assisted suicide? Does a state that bans PAS violate the Constitution? Does a state that permits PAS violate the Constitution? Does a patient's death that is hastened by the use of drugs to relieve pain and suffering, even though that is not the physician's intent, constitute a case of PAS?

FIVE

PHYSICIAN-ASSISTED SUICIDE AND THE SUPREME COURT: 1997

AMONG THOSE JUSTICES joining the majority opinion of the U.S. Supreme Court in June 1990—denying Nancy Cruzan the right to die—had been the out-spoken Antonin Scalia. Justice Scalia did not merely agree with the Court's decision. He further stated that he "would have preferred that we announce, clearly and promptly, that the federal courts have no business in this field" and that it was up to the individual states to prevent suicide and to preserve life at all costs."

Yet, surprisingly, seven years later, in 1997, the high court agreed to hear two cases that dealt directly with the subject of physician-assisted suicide, or PAS. The two cases—known as *Washington* v. *Glucksberg* and *Vacco* v. *Quill*—were essentially similar in nature. Both dealt with the requests of physicians, the first in the state of Washington and the second in the state of New York, to treat terminally ill competent patients who had specifically asked for a means of ending their lives.

As a result of the similarity of the cases, the Supreme Court elected to hear them in tandem on January 8, 1997. The Court's decision was rendered on June 26, 1997.

WASHINGTON V. GLUCKSBERG
(521 U.S. 702)

Although the state of Washington had a long-standing ban on physician-assisted suicide, practicing physician Dr. Harold Glucksberg, along with four other members of his profession, sought to challenge the ban on behalf of three terminally ill patients.

One of the patients was dying of breast cancer that had spread rapidly throughout her body; the second, who was dying of AIDS, had lost most of his eyesight and was repeatedly gripped by severe seizures; the third had to live in an oxygen tent due to terminal emphysema. All three patients were mentally competent.

The original suit was brought in the U.S. District Court for Western Washington in 1994 under the case name *Compassion in Dying, et al., v. Washington*.

Compassion in Dying was an organization that had been formed in Seattle in 1993. Its mission was to provide counsel and direct assistance to the mentally competent terminally ill and to challenge state laws that banned PAS.

Although the suit failed in its first attempt to have Washington State law declared unconstitutional, it succeeded a second time around in a Federal District Court in the state. This decision, however, was overturned by Washington's Ninth Circuit Court of Appeals with a vote of two judges to one.

Compassion in Dying, et al. attorneys then demanded a rehearing in the appeals court on the ground that the divided roster of judges had been too small and was religiously prejudiced against PAS. The rehearing, with eleven judges, proved successful for the plaintiffs, resulting in a vote of 8 to 3 in their favor. The majority agreed that the Washington ban on PAS violated the "liberty" and "due process" rights of the Fourteenth Amendment. ["No State shall . . . deprive any person of life, liberty, or property, without due process of law."]

In other words, a state law prohibiting liberty, or the right to make personal decisions, as in the 1973 *Roe* v. *Wade* Supreme Court decision, was unconstitutional according to the Ninth Circuit Court of Appeals.

The state of Washington, unwilling to accept the decision that it was in violation of the U.S. Constitution, then turned around and brought suit in the U.S. Supreme Court against Glucksberg. The case before the High Court was thus renamed for the now-plaintiff against the now-defendant, or the accused, and was titled *Washington* v. *Glucksberg*. By the time the case was heard in January 1997, all of the original terminally ill patients had died, in some cases having been helped by a family member or through having committed suicide. Their cases went unresolved by the Court.

VACCO V. *QUILL* (521 U.S. 793), COMPANION CASE TO *GLUCKSBERG*

Timothy E. Quill was a New York State-licensed physician in Rochester, New York, where he was also a professor of medicine and psychiatry at the University of Rochester.

As in the *Glucksberg* case, and also starting in 1994, Quill allied himself with other physicians and a trio of plaintiff-patients to challenge the constitutionality of the New York State law banning PAS. The original case title *Quill* v. *Vacco* was derived from the name of the New York State attorney general, Dennis C. Vacco, who was cast in the role of defendant.

Among Quill's patients who had requested medical help to end their lives were a seventy-six-year-old woman who was dying of thyroid cancer, and two younger men who were dying of the ravages of AIDS.

The suit was first brought to trial in 1994 in the U.S. District Court of the Southern District of New York. The

NEW YORK STATE ATTORNEY GENERAL DENNIS C. VACCO WAS THE DEFENDANT
IN A CASE BROUGHT BY DR. TIMOTHY E. QUILL TO CHALLENGE THE CONSTITU-
TIONALITY OF THE LAW AGAINST PHYSICIAN-ASSISTED SUICIDE.

judge ruled in favor of New York State. He argued that the ban on PAS was constitutional because, in his view, patients had no constitutional right to assisted suicide.

Quill and his associates appealed the decision and the case was then heard in 1995 in New York City by three judges of the Second Circuit Court of Appeals. This time the decision favored Quill on the ground that denying some patients PAS via a lethal prescription and allowing others to die through the withdrawal of life support was a violation of the equal protection clause of the Fourteenth Amendment. ["No State shall . . . deny to any person within its jurisdiction the equal protection of the laws."]

In other words, the court felt that there were currently two means of hastening death for competent patients. One was the withdrawal of respirators, feeding tubes, or other life support systems at the specific request of the patient. This means was legal under the Patient Self-Determination Act, which took effect in 1991 and gave competent patients (in medical institutions receiving federal funds) the right to refuse treatment.

The other means was the writing of a prescription for a lethal substance to hasten death, which was illegal in New York State. However, since patients in both categories could be suffering equally in the face of imminent and inevitable death, the court asserted that the state was wrong to rule that, while one means was legal, the other was illegal. Therefore New York was denying its inhabitants the "equal protection of the laws" as dictated by the Constitution.

HOW WASHINGTON AND NEW YORK PAS CASES REACHED THE HIGHEST COURT

Following *Cruzan* v. *Missouri* in 1989 to 1990, it had appeared fairly clear that the U.S. Supreme Court would henceforth leave right-to-die cases in the hands of the individual states. However, the decisions in favor of the constitutionality of PAS in the Ninth Circuit Court of Appeals (re Washington) and the Second Circuit Court of Appeals (re New York) changed the picture for the entire nation and became a matter that had to be resolved by the highest court in the land, due to the nature of the circuit court system.

January 8, 1997, saw the Supreme Court hearing, in tandem, of the two cases that had been brought against the states of Washington and New York in an attempt to overturn their laws prohibiting PAS. The two states where suit had been brought were not the only ones involved because jurisdiction of the Second and Ninth Circuit Courts of Appeal reached beyond their boundaries into other states.

The procedure for the day would be that each of the cases would be given a full hour for argument, with one immediately following the other. Dozens of *amicus curiae* or "friend of the court" briefs had been filed by supporters of the state laws prohibiting PAS and by those opposing them. Included were religious groups, medical associations, medical ethicists, legislators, and philosophers.

In the forefront of those opposing PAS were the Roman Catholic Church, Orthodox Jewish groups, and a militant right-to-life group of disabled people known as Not Dead Yet. Among those groups favoring state laws permitting PAS were Compassion in Dying and the radical Hemlock Society (formed in 1980 in California), which advocated assisted dying and even distributed how-to-die information.

The brunt of the arguments heard before the Court was as follows. Attorneys representing the states of Washington and New York indicated that it was in the state's interest to protect life and that the terminally ill had no constitutional right to demand that a physician assist them in hastening their deaths.

The attorneys for the physicians and their terminal patients countered with the argument that there was a

How the circuit courts work

In early times in the United States, it was easier for a judge to go to the place of a court hearing than for the applicants and their lawyers to come to him. So judges rode a circuit that covered a specific territory.

Today the United States is divided into twelve circuit courts covering the entire nation and its territories. The Second Circuit Court of Appeals, for example, covers not only New York but also the states of Connecticut and Vermont. The Ninth Circuit Court of Appeals covers not only the state of Washington but also a number of other western states.

Therefore, rulings made in these courts apply beyond the boundaries of the states where the original suit took place. In fact, combining the pro-physician-assisted suicide (PAS) findings of the Second and Ninth Circuit Courts of Appeal meant that nearly one quarter of the United States would have legal access to physician-assisted suicide!

While the United States Supreme Court went through the necessary steps of scheduling the case for a final and irrevocable decision, it issued a court order putting PAS on hold. No doctor in any of the states included in the Second and Ninth Circuits was permitted to help terminally ill patients to end their lives.

protected liberty interest in the Constitution that permitted PAS. Further, it was discriminatory to make relief
from suffering available to some patients through the
withdrawal of life support, while forcing those who were
not on life support to endure agonies that could only be
ended via a lethal prescription.

As was usual in Supreme Court cases, the justices
broke into the arguments of the attorneys on both sides
with questions and comments. Justice Antonin Scalia
asked Kathryn Tucker, who was arguing the Washington
case for PAS, "Why should that decision [to request PAS]
if it's competent, reasoned, and deliberated, why should it
be limited to physical pain? What—about the patient who
has terrible emotional suffering in life and just says life is
not worth it anymore? . . . You would not allow assisted
suicide in that case, I take it?"

Tucker replied, "No, Your Honor."

Justice Ruth Bader Ginsburg asked Tucker, "Isn't
there the possibility of a person saying, gee, I really
thought I wanted it [PAS] yesterday, but today I don't?"

Tucker admitted that there was such a possibility and
inserted the thought that a state permitting PAS would
probably want to impose a waiting period.

Laurence H. Tribe, the attorney representing the New
York physicians advocating PAS, was asked by Justice John
Paul Stevens, "Tell us what you think the liberty interest is?"

Tribe responded, "The liberty interest in this case is
. . . when facing imminent and inevitable death, not to be
forced by the government to endure a degree of pain and
suffering that one can relieve only by being completely
unconscious. Not to be . . . a creature of the state but to
have some voice in the question of how much pain one is
really going through."

Justice Scalia, who believed in a strictly literal interpretation of the Constitution as it was originally written,

quipped, "All of this is in the Constitution? . . . You see, this is lovely philosophy. But you want us to frame a Constitutional rule on the basis of that?"

supreme court decides washington and new york cases re PAS

While the Glucksberg and Quill cases dealt, in terms of the Constitution, with the Fourteenth Amendment issues of "due process of law" and "equal protection of the laws," there were also many broad concerns regarding life in twentieth century America that were addressed.

The queries and comments of the justices, and the arguments and responses of attorneys on both sides, reflected the changing attitudes in society at large, as well as in medicine, religion, government, and ethics.

As Linda Greenhouse, Supreme Court reporter for the *New York Times*, wrote:

> this was a Supreme Court session notable for the proportion of plain English that was spoken. The Justices wanted theory but they were also hungry for facts. They sat as judges but appeared to feel themselves very much participants, on a human level, in a far-reaching societal debate. "This is an issue every one of us faces, young and old, male and female, whatever it might be," Justice Sandra Day O'Connor said at one point. And Justice Ginsburg, whose mother died of cervical cancer at the age of forty-seven, said, "Most of us have parents and other loved ones who have been through the dying process and we've thought about these things."

However, in spite of the openness of the hearings and the expressed sympathies of some of the justices for the scope of the right-to-die problem, the entire Court came down on the side of the legality of the PAS bans in the states of Washington and New York.

In a unanimous vote of 9 to 0, the Court held that both state laws were constitutional and did not violate either the "due process" or the "equal protection" guarantees of the Fourteenth Amendment.

Chief Justice William Rehnquist delivered the opinion of the Court, in which he wrote that no liberty right to PAS existed in the Constitution and that, moreover, American history and tradition dictated that suicide and assisted suicide were criminal acts, as they were in many other parts of the world. Justice Rehnquist's exact words concerning the former were, "Our decisions lead us to conclude that the asserted 'right' to assistance in committing suicide is not a fundamental liberty interest protected by the Due Process Clause."

The other justices wrote concurring opinions. Justices Antonin Scalia and Clarence Thomas, both deeply conservative, agreed strongly with Justice Rehnquist. In her concurrence, Justice Sandra Day O'Connor pointed out that most suffering patients had the opportunity to obtain relief through medicines that might also hasten death.

This element of treatment of the terminally ill, also known as the "double effect," had been openly discussed at the hearings. When a doctor increases the level of morphine, in order to make a suffering patient more comfortable, and that increase results in the patient dying sooner, does that constitute a case of PAS? No answers were given to this murky question at the hearings, as "double effect" was not the issue at stake.

Although he joined the majority opinion, one of the Court's most liberal justices, John Paul Stevens, declared that he found inconsistencies in the state of Washington's ban on assisted suicide because Washington also had a law

CHIEF JUSTICE WILLIAM REHNQUIST DELIVERED THE 9 TO 0 OPINION OF THE
SUPREME COURT IN THE GLUCKSBERG AND QUILL CASES—TO UPHOLD THE BAN
AGAINST PHYSICIAN-ASSISTED SUICIDES.

legalizing capital punishment.

As a result, Stevens wrote, "A state, like Washington,
that has authorized the death penalty and thereby has
concluded that the sanctity of human life does not
require that it always be preserved, must acknowledge
that there are situations in which an interest in hastening
death is legitimate. Indeed not only is that interest some-
times legitimate, I am also convinced that there are times
when it is entitled to constitutional protection."

Justice Stevens also made reference to the Nancy Cruzan case in writing his opinion. He pointed out that the now-deceased plaintiff patients in the Washington and New York cases "may in fact have had a liberty interest even stronger than Nancy Cruzan's because, not only were they terminally ill, they were suffering constant and severe pain."

Justices David H. Souter and Steven G. Breyer also took a more positive view than did Rehnquist and the conservatives of the potential for a right to die. Both justices agreed with the conservatives that state legislatures rather than the courts were the proper decision-making bodies. There, voters could directly express their feelings regarding PAS. Justice Souter preferred not to call PAS a "right to commit suicide with another's assistance," but a "right to die with dignity."

Already, in fact, one state—Oregon—had experimented with trying to pass a state law legalizing PAS and had attained success by a slim margin of 52 percent in favor and 48 percent against. The proposal that was voted on for the first time on November 8, 1994, was called Oregon Measure 16. It would come to be known as the Death with Dignity Act.

THE OREGON DEATH WITH DIGNITY ACT

The early 1990s saw attempts by the states of Washington and California to pass a Death with Dignity Act. But both failed to win the voters' approval by margins of 54 percent opposed and 46 percent in favor. In addition to the opposition encountered from religious and medical groups, many people were fearful that governments might take over control of the lives of those ailing and unfit individuals who did not want to die, as in Hitler's Germany in the late 1930s.

Clearly, it was necessary to include in any such

ALTHOUGH ASSOCIATE JUSTICE JOHN PAUL STEVENS JOINED THE COURT'S
DECISION AGAINST PHYSICIAN-ASSISTED SUICIDE, HE DID POINT OUT THE
INCONSISTENCY BETWEEN BANNING ASSISTED SUICIDE AND KEEPING CAPITAL
PUNISHMENT LEGAL.

measure safeguards that would limit PAS only to those
patients who were fully competent, terminally ill (with
only six months to live), and suffering severe or unbearable pain or discomfort.

There would also have to be a system of checks and

balances among the physicians involved in the PAS request, the patient, and the patient's next of kin. Patients who were emotionally unstable, depressed, or had had longtime suicidal tendencies without qualifying medical conditions could not be candidates for PAS.

The Oregon Death with Dignity Act was scheduled to take effect one month after Measure 16 was passed, on December 5, 1994. However, strong opponents of the new statute, including the National Right to Life Committee, blocked its implementation just hours before December 5 dawned.

Declaring that the new law was unconstitutional because it denied residents of Oregon protection from suicide and manslaughter, the plaintiffs got a federal district court judge to have it put on hold. Supporters of the law immediately launched an appeal.

Nevertheless, three years passed before Oregonians had a functioning Death with Dignity Act. During that time, challenges to its constitutionality continued. But in February 1997, the Ninth Circuit Court of Appeals denied the plaintiffs' claim that the Act was unconstitutional.

For supporters, there was one more hurdle to overcome. Opponents of the act demanded that Oregon voters be given a chance to cast their ballots in favor of repealing Measure 16. The repeal bill known as Measure 51 was voted on in the fall of 1997 and was defeated by a margin of 60 percent against repeal versus 40 percent favoring it. In other words, the 1997 repeal of the Death with Dignity Act was opposed even more strongly than the 1994 vote by which the measure had originally passed.

The Oregon Death with Dignity Act has been in effect since October 27, 1997. Its opponents predicted that mass deaths would follow the legalization of PAS. However, figures kept by the Department of Human Services of the state of Oregon indicate that was not so.

THE REQUIREMENTS OF OREGON'S DEATH WITH DIGNITY ACT

To obtain a prescription for a lethal medication from an Oregon physician, an Oregon resident must meet the following criteria. Under the Oregon law, euthanasia, in which a physician directly administers a lethal drug, is illegal.

The patient must be an Oregon resident at least eighteen years old.

The patient must have been diagnosed with a terminal illness that will lead to death in six months.

The patient must make both oral and written requests for assistance in dying, separated by at least fifteen days.

The patient must give the physician a signed written request that has been witnessed by two persons, one not a relative.

The prescribing doctor and a consulting physician must confirm the patient's terminal diagnosis and prognosis.

The prescribing doctor and a consulting physician must determine that the patient is capable and acting voluntarily.

The patient must be referred for counseling if either the prescribing doctor or the consulting physician believes that the patient's judgment is impaired by a psychiatric or psychological disorder.

The prescribing doctor must inform the patient of alternatives to assisted suicide, such as comfort care, pain control, and hospice care.

The prescribing doctor must notify the patient and the patient's next of kin that the patient can change the decision at any time.

OREGON IS THE ONE STATE IN WHICH PHYSICIAN-ASSISTED SUICIDE IS LEGAL. THOUGH CHALLENGED THROUGH THE YEARS SINCE ITS 1994 PASSAGE, IT REMAINS A LEGAL OPTION.

Between 1999 and 2005, 246 individuals died in Oregon as a result of ingesting a lethal medication prescribed by a physician. In the same time period, there were 74,967 other patients who were dying from the same underlying diseases who did not choose PAS.

THE CONVICTION OF DR. KEVORKIAN

Throughout the 1900s, American society grappled with the issue of the right to die. From 1906, when the state of Ohio attempted to draft the first euthanasia bill, to 1997, when the state of Oregon succeeded in implementing its Death with Dignity Act, physician-assisted suicide met with conflicting responses in the legislatures and in the courts.

The U.S. Supreme Court accepted only three of the many cases dealing with the right to die that had been brought up for hearings over the century—*Cruzan* v. *Missouri* (1989–1990), *Washington* v. *Glucksberg* (1997), and *Vacco* v. *Quill* (1997). And, in view of the 1997 unanimous decision of the Court in upholding the constitutionality of the PAS bans in Washington and New York, it appeared unlikely that it would take on any more such cases.

One of the many petitioners who attempted unsuccessfully to appeal a right-to-die case to the Supreme Court was Dr. Jack Kevorkian, who had first come to public attention in 1990, when he administered PAS to a fifty-four-year-old Oregon woman, Janet Adkins, afflicted with early-onset Alzheimer's disease.

In the eight years that followed, Kevorkian was responsible for the deaths of more than one hundred patients via assisted suicide. Although he was charged with murder several times in the state of Michigan, where he practiced, he was not convicted due to either mistrials or dismissal of charges, largely because Michigan law was unclear on the subject of PAS.

Kevorkian's next step, however, proved to be lethal to his practice as well as his patient. On September 17, 1998, the man who had been nicknamed "Dr. Death" directly administered a fatal dose of medication to fifty-two-year-old Thomas Youk, who was suffering from ALS, otherwise known as Lou Gehrig's disease.

In an effort to publicize his work, Kevorkian had videotaped both Youk's request to die as well as the doctor giving Youk the fatal injection. Heretofore, Kevorkian had prepared the lethal injection or inhalant, and the patient had self-administered it by pushing the device on Kevorkian's "suicide machine" that would release it. In Youk's case, however, it was clear that Kevorkian was performing active euthanasia rather than providing PAS. Youk may have been too disabled to operate the machine.

Kevorkian had often appeared on television and even gave the tape of a death he had provided to an ALS sufferer to CBS's *60 Minutes* television program. The showing of the tape, in November 1998, prompted the state of Michigan to charge Kevorkian with second-degree murder. He was convicted in 1999 to serve a ten- to twenty-five-year jail sentence. His request for a parole in June 2007 was granted on the condition that he not assist in any future suicides.

Kevorkian's trial in March 1999, at which he insisted on pleading his own case, resulted in his conviction. On April 13, 1999, he was sentenced, on a reduced charge of second-degree murder, to serve a prison term of ten to twenty-five years.

Three years later, in April 2002, an attorney for Kevorkian asked the state Supreme Court of Michigan to grant his client a new trial on the ground that Kevorkian's conviction had been unconstitutional. This request was denied.

Kevorkian then turned to the U.S. Supreme Court. In October 2002, the highest court in the land refused to take his case on appeal. Kevorkian, who was born on May 26, 1928, and was then age seventy-four, stated that he expected to die in prison while serving out even the minimal ten years of his term.

SIX

THE RIGHT TO DIE
LIVES ON

THE U.S. supreme court's refusal to get involved in right-to-die cases, on behalf of either physicians accused of euthanasia, such as Dr. Jack Kevorkian, or of patients and their families, became increasingly evident in the opening years of the 2000s.

"Supreme Court Refuses to Hear the Schiavo Case." This was the heading of a report appearing in the *New York Times* on March 25, 2005. Nor was the high court's denial in the "Schiavo case" its first. The parents of a young woman named Terri Schiavo, who had fallen into a permanent vegetative state in 1990, had been petitioning the Court since 2001, with no success.

"Terri," as Schiavo became popularly known in the media, was born Theresa Marie Schindler on December 3, 1963, in Pennsylvania. She grew up in a Philadelphia suburb, the eldest of three children in a religious Roman Catholic family.

As a teenager Terri was considerably overweight. At 5'3", she weighed 250 pounds. In her senior year at a private Catholic high school, she began to diet and appeared to have developed an eating disorder. Just short of her twenty-first birthday, in November 1984, Terri Schindler married Michael Schiavo, whom she had met while both

TERRI SCHIAVO AND HER MOTHER, MARY SCHINDLER, ARE PICTURED AT TERRI'S HOSPITAL BED IN 2003.

were students at a community college in Pennsylvania.

In 1986, the couple moved to Florida, followed a few months later by Terri's family, her parents and two younger siblings. Terri had found work as a claims clerk for an insurance company, while her husband, Michael, had gotten a job as a restaurant manager.

By this time, Terri, 5'4", weighed only 110 pounds. But she was still trying to lose more weight. Her husband and her friends were not unaware of her practice of bingeing, or overeating, and then purging by means of vomiting and using laxatives. This pattern, known as *bulimia nervosa*, was apparently an extension of the eating disorder that had begun in Terri's teen years.

In 1989, Terri and Michael Schiavo sought medical help in conceiving a child, and Terri began receiving fertility treatments. As a lawsuit against the obstetrician who was treating Terri later revealed, the doctor had failed to do a thorough check of her eating disorder, which had resulted in a serious potassium imbalance in her blood.

Early on the morning of February 25, 1990, Terri Schiavo collapsed in the St. Petersburg, Florida, apartment where she and Michael lived. Michael Schiavo called 911. Paramedics and firefighters found Terri face down and unconscious in what appeared to be a case of cardiac arrest. She could not be revived and was taken to St. Petersburg's Humana Northside Hospital in a coma.

Terri was intubated (a tube was inserted into her trachea, or windpipe), given a tracheotomy (a surgical opening made into the trachea), and put on a respirator.

Doctors also inserted a feeding tube into her stomach through the abdominal wall, a surgical procedure known as a PEG (percutaneous endoscopic gastrostomy). This was the same type of feeding tube that Nancy Cruzan had received soon after her car crash in 1983.

Also, like Nancy Cruzan, Terri Schiavo's brain had suffered the effects of anoxia (the deprivation of oxygen) during the time between her collapse at home and her resuscitation at the hospital. The hospital diagnosis was that she had suffered anoxic brain damage, along with respiratory failure, due to cardiac arrest, or heart stoppage, as a result of an abnormally low potassium blood level.

According to *USA Today*, medical reports attributed Terri's potassium imbalance to the fact that "she apparently has been trying to keep her weight down with dieting by herself, drinking liquids most of the time during the day and drinking about 10-15 glasses of [caffeinated] iced tea."

After two and a half months at Humana Northside Hospital, Terri emerged from a coma into PVS, or a persistent vegetative state, with its typical sleep-awake cycles in which the eyes may appear to follow movement and the brainstem reflexes of moans and grimaces may be evident. However, as in all PVS syndromes, there is no awareness of one's self or one's surroundings. There is no ability to use language or to comprehend it, no other means of communication, no bodily response to ordinary stimuli, and there is incontinence.

Disbelieving the hopelessness of Terri's condition, resulting from the anoxic brain damage that had destroyed the cortex, or thinking part of her brain, Terri's husband, Michael, and her parents now began a series of attempts to rehabilitate her. On June 18, 1990, with the consent of Terri's parents, a judge appointed Michael her guardian.

Starting on May 12, 1990, when Terri was discharged from Humana, she was transferred to a series of rehabilitation facilities, was sent home for a brief time, was taken by her husband to California for an experimental brain-stimulation treatment that failed, and back to yet another brain-injury center in Florida.

As the years passed, a rift developed between Terri's husband, Michael, and Terri's parents. Michael, who had obtained a degree in respiration therapy and in nursing in order to care for Terri and be better informed about her condition, began to agree with her physicians that her condition was irreversible. Also, although Terri had left no written directives, Michael recalled several occasions, with other witnesses present, when Terri had declared that she would not want to be kept alive by artificial means. As a result, in May 1998, more than eight years after her collapse, Michael, as Terri's guardian, filed a petition with the Pinellas County Circuit Court for authorization to have Terri's feeding tube removed.

Terri's parents, Mary and Bob Schindler, on the other hand, persisted in their belief that Terri responded to them on their frequent visits to the nursing home in which she was a patient. They asserted that she smiled, wept, stared at them lovingly, and even attempted to speak to them. In due course, they filmed a series of videos showing Terri in what appeared to be expressions of recognition and wordless efforts at communication.

Nearly two years passed before Michael Schiavo's case went to trial. In February 2000, the circuit court judge, George W. Greer, rendered his verdict. Two issues were involved. Was Terri Schiavo in PVS and would it have been her own wish to have the feeding tube removed?

In the matter of Terri's medical condition, Judge Greer enlisted the testimony of physicians who exhibited CAT scans of Terri's brain showing the almost complete absence of a cerebral cortex and its vacancy replaced with spinal fluid. He found therefore "beyond all doubt that Theresa Marie Schiavo is in a persistent vegetative state" and "has no hope of ever regaining consciousness." The movements that Terri's parents felt showed evidence of consciousness, Judge Greer affirmed, "are reflexive and predicated on brain stem activity alone."

Judge Greer further stated that "without the feeding tube she will die in seven to fourteen days" but that "the unrebutted medical testimony before this court is that such death would be painless."

Concerning Terri's orally expressed end-of-life wishes, Judge Greer found "that Terri Schiavo did make

PINELLAS COUNTY CIRCUIT JUDGE GEORGE GREER SIGNED THE ORDER
ALLOWING FOR THE REMOVAL OF TERRI SCHIAVO'S FEEDING TUBE.

statements which are creditable and reliable with regard
to her intention given the situation at hand" and those
statements rose "to the level of clear and convincing evidence to this court."

On February 11, 2000, Judge Greer ordered that Terri
Schiavo's feeding tube, based on the petition of her husband, should be removed. But, unlike the cases of Karen

Quinlan and Nancy Cruzan, in which the families of the PVS patients were of a single mind, the dispute between Terri's parents and her husband and guardian would continue. Court orders would be defied, appeals to undo them would be filed, and right-to-life advocates—including the governor of Florida, the U.S. Congress, and the nation's president himself—would become publicly involved.

THe Five-Year STrUGGLe TO ResOLVe THe scHIaVO Case: 2000–2005

The immediate reaction of the Schindlers to Judge Greer's order of February 2000, was to file an appeal with Florida's District Court of Appeal, during which time Terri's feeding tube remained connected and her condition was unaltered.

A year passed in this fashion, and on January 24, 2001, the appellate court rendered its decision. It upheld the opinion of the Pinellas County Circuit Court. Terri Schiavo's cerebral cortex, the thinking part of her brain, had been replaced with spinal fluid, a deterioration that was beyond medical treatment. Her expressed past opinion on the subject of not wanting to live with the support of tubes had been clear and convincing. Thus the year-old order of Judge Greer was to be carried out without delay.

Once again the Schindlers sought to appeal the verdict, applying to both the Florida Supreme Court and the U.S. Supreme Court. Both higher courts refused to hear the case. On April 24, 2001, Terri's supply of artificial nutrition and hydration (ANH) was cut off. But the Schindlers obtained an emergency injunction, claiming that they had new medical opinions and a new therapy to present pertaining to their daughter's case, and two days later Terri's tube feeding was restored.

The pattern of appeals and upheld decisions favoring

Michael Schiavo, countered by stays of action and efforts to introduce new evidence on the part of the Schindlers, continued until the second attempted removal of Terri's feeding tube on October 15, 2003.

This time the Schindlers elicited and received support from Florida's right-to-life Republican governor Jeb Bush, the brother of President George W. Bush. With the emergency passage of a bill in the state legislature that became known as "Terri's Law," Governor Bush managed to have Terri's feeding tube reinserted on October 21, 2003, only six days after its October 15 removal.

Although "Terri's Law" temporarily restored Terri Schiavo's feeding tube in October 2003, it was doomed to fail. The original court order for the tube to be disconnected still stood and, in 2004, two court hearings took place, both of which determined that "Terri's Law" was unconstitutional.

In the first case, Michael Schiavo sued Governor Jeb Bush in Pinellas County Circuit Court on the constitutionality of the law the governor had instigated and signed.

On May 5, 2004, the presiding judge affirmed that "Terri's Law" was in violation of the constitutional separation of powers among the executive, legislative, and judicial branches of government.

Governor Bush (the executive branch) had not only infringed on the jurisdiction of the courts (the judicial branch), but he had assumed power over the Florida state houses (the legislative branch) by imposing policy in the form of the emergency measure known as "Terri's Law."

Jeb Bush responded to this verdict by filing for an appeal that was heard in the Florida Supreme Court. *Bush* v. *Schiavo* went before the court on August 31, 2004, with lawyers for both the governor of Florida and Michael Schiavo offering oral arguments to the seven justices who heard the case.

RIGHT-TO-LIFE ORGANIZER RANDALL TERRY WAS ONE OF THE LEADERS OF THE FIGHT TO KEEP TERRI SCHIAVO ALIVE.

In the decision rendered on September 23, 2004, the justices unanimously upheld the lower court ruling. "Terri's Law" was unconstitutional. The governor had overstepped the boundaries of the democratic system of the United States. He had also, according to the Florida Supreme Court, failed to consider the wishes of the patient, Terri Schiavo, as expressed prior to her collapse and as accepted by all previous court rulings.

In December 2004, Jeb Bush made an additional stab at getting a ruling on the constitutionality of "Terri's Law." He asked the Supreme Court to review the two previous negative decisions. On January 24, 2005, the high court responded. It refused to review the case. Thus no impediments remained to prevent the original order for the removal of Terri's feeding tube from being carried out.

On the afternoon of March 18, 2005—one day after the Supreme Court had yet again declined to review the case—Terri Schiavo's feeding tube was removed for the third and final time. There was an immediate reaction from Operation Rescue, other antiabortion and right-to-life groups, and the religious right, including Southern Baptists, Roman Catholics, and other conservative Christians. Protesters with signs invoking biblical commands against killing held noisy vigils behind police barriers.

Now, President George W. Bush entered the fray directly. In a statement on March 21, 2005, the nation's highest elected official said, "In cases like this one, where there are serious questions and substantial doubts, our society, our laws, and our courts should have a presumption in favor of life. This presumption is especially critical for those like Terri Schiavo, who live at the mercy of others."

In other words, the meticulously arrived-at scientific findings of the medical community and the legally confirmed wishes of the patient herself were apparently of no

"Terri's Law" and the RIGHT-TO-LIFE Campaign

The second attempt to remove Terri Schiavo's feeding tube, as ordered by the courts, drew enormous protests from conservative activists who had been gearing up for demonstrations in the vicinity of Hospice House Woodside in Pinellas Park, Florida, where Terri was now being cared for.

Among the right-to-life leaders was Randall Terry, the founder of Operation Rescue, an anti-abortion organization that had a history of harassing abortion clinics and advocating the murder of abortion doctors. Others prominent in the movement to "rescue" Terri were rightists who included members of the clergy, conservative talk-show hosts, and extremist political figures.

The groups they inspired set up twenty-four-hour vigils, shouted slogans and quotes from the Bible, and waved signs that read "Michael Schiavo is a murderer," and "God numbers our days—not man." A motor home stationed near Hospice House Woodside served as a command post for the coordination of "rescue" actions. To all of this Terri's parents had given their approval.

The general goal of the conservative activists was to remind the American people that all life is precious regardless of its quality (a position questioned by many patients, physicians, and bioethicists). Also (despite medical opinion to the contrary) the activists declared that death by dehydration and starvation, even in PVS— and therefore unconscious—patients, was painful and agonizing.

The immediate goal of the radical right was to pressure Florida's governor to stop the removal of Terri's feeding tube, and their efforts were successful. On

October 20-21, 2003, "Terri's Law" hastily passed the state legislature and Governor Jeb Bush signed it into law. Quite simply "Terri's Law" stated that, as of October 15, 2003, Florida's governor had the *one time only* authority to issue a stay of the feeding tube's court-ordered removal. Although President George W. Bush stated that he believed his brother had done the right thing, it was evident even before "Terri's Law" had been passed in the Florida legislature that it was unconstitutional. Under the constitutional system of checks and balances, legislation cannot overturn a judicial ruling that is subject to review by a higher court. Only the higher court possesses that authority.

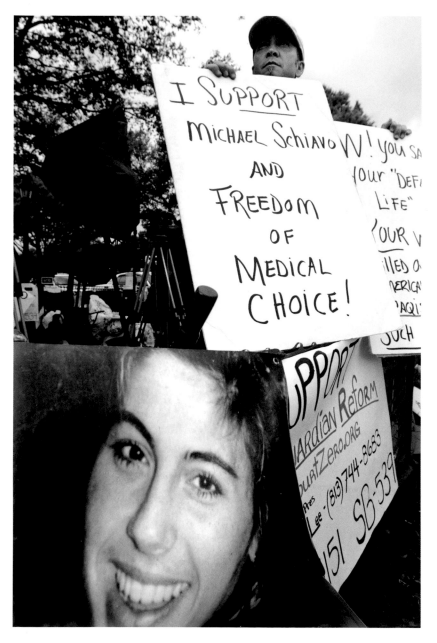

MANY PEOPLE SUPPORTED MICHAEL SCHIAVO'S FIGHT TO HAVE HIS WIFE'S
FEEDING TUBE REMOVED.

validity and lay beyond the consideration of President George Bush. As a result, the president made an official attempt to take the matter out of the hands of the state courts and into Congress, hoping to obtain a federal court order to have Terri's feeding tube reinserted.

In an unprecedented emergency session on a matter not of national significance, a sprinkling of members of Congress met on Sunday, March 20, during the Easter recess and approved the president's measure. That same day the president returned to Washington from his Texas ranch to sign it into law.

Would the jurisdiction of the U.S. court system give way to presidential opinion based on a political agenda and personal religious conviction? The answer was no. On March 22, 2005, the federal district court to which the case was referred refused to order the reinsertion of the tube. On March 23, a federal appeals court affirmed the decision of the federal district court. And on March 24, the U.S. Supreme Court declined, for the final time, to review the Schiavo case.

All efforts to violate the oft-reaffirmed decisions of the Florida state courts had failed. Judge Greer's original decision held and Terri Schiavo now had only a week left to live.

TERRI SCHIAVO'S DEATH AND ITS AFTERMATH

Shortly after 9 AM on March 31, 2005, Terri Schiavo, age forty-one, died peacefully in her bed at Hospice House Woodside, with her husband, Michael, at her side.

Contrary to the claims of conservative activists opposed to the removal of the feeding tube, Terri did not suffer agonizing pain and distress due to starvation and dehydration. Dr. Sean Morrison, a professor of geriatrics and palliative care at Mount Sinai School of Medicine in

IN THE CIRCUIT COURT FOR PINELLAS COUNTY, FLORIDA
PROBATE DIVISION

IN RE: THE GUARDIANSHIP OF
THERESA MARIE SCHIAVO,   File No. 90-2908-GD-003
Incapacitated.

MICHAEL SCHIAVO,

                 Petitioner,
vs.

ROBERT SCHINDLER and MARY
SCHINDLER,

              Respondents.

ORDER

THIS CAUSE came before the Court for hearing on February 23, 2005, on Respondents' Motion for Emergency Stay of Execution of February 11, 2000, Order to Remove Theresa Schiavo's Nutrition and Hydration filed on February 15, 2005. David C. Gibbs, III, Esq, appeared for the Respondents and George J. Felos, Esq, appeared for the Petitioner.

The Second District Court of Appeal issued its standard Mandate in this case on February 22, 2005, and Respondents now contend that an indefinite stay should be granted by this Court based on (1) appellate review of this Court's Order of February 11, 2005; (2) the Petition to Remove the Guardian pending before this Court; and (3) their intention to file a petition for a writ of certiorari with the United States Supreme Court to review the orders of this Court and of the Second District Court of Appeal on the effect of a papal pronouncement. In addition to the stay, Respondents also ask that the Court prevent the Petitioner from removing Theresa Schiavo's nutrition and hydration without further order of the Court.

THIS RULING ISSUED IN A FLORIDA COURT ON MARCH 18, 2005, DENIES THE SCHINDLERS' PETITION AND ORDERS THE REMOVAL OF TERRI SCHIAVO'S FEEDING TUBE.

New York, explained that PVS patients "don't recognize food. If you put food in their mouth, it would sit there until they took a breath, and then that food would go down into the lungs."

Nor would a patient who had been on a feeding tube for fifteen years have been able to swallow water by mouth without taking it into the lungs and, in effect, drowning. Yet, among the religious conservative right-to-life Protesters outside the hospice, there were those activists who attempted to run the police barriers with glasses of water for Terri.

As further explained by Morrison and other medical experts, Terri Schiavo lost the ability to experience pain when her higher brain function was destroyed through the loss of oxygen in 1990. And even conscious patients who willfully give up food and water as death approaches do not experience hunger pangs and extreme thirst as do those individuals who have been eating and drinking regularly and are suddenly deprived.

In fact, conscious patients who make the decision to give up food and water in the end stage of life experience an initial euphoria followed by a natural shutting down of the body's vital organs.

Although the Schindler family wanted Terri's body to be buried in a Catholic cemetery in Florida, her husband and guardian chose cremation preceded by an autopsy. The purpose of the autopsy was to confirm the nature of Terri's condition and to disprove claims leveled at Michael that he had physically abused Terri prior to her collapse in 1990.

The findings of the Pinellas County medical examiner in charge of the postmortem investigation of Terri's death were as follows. As a direct result of anoxia, Terri's severely damaged brain was atrophied and was half its normal weight. Terri was blind because her brain's vision center was dead. Terri's illness was consistent with the diagnosis of PVS and was completely irreversible. Terri had not been strangled or suffered any traumatic injuries at the time of her hospital admission in 1990.

The release of Terri Schiavo's autopsy results on June 15, 2005, appeared to do little to change the minds of those who had been opposed to the removal of her feeding tube. The Schindlers continued to insist that Terri had been cognizant of them and responsive to their presence at all times. Jeb Bush told the Schindlers, his religious conservative supporters, and the media that he was heartbroken at Terri's death and regretted not having been able to violate a court order. And President George W. Bush urged all those who honored Terri Schiavo to work to "build a culture of life."

Tom DeLay, then Republican House of Representatives majority leader (who was forced to resign in 2006 on a personal ethics matter) issued the following ominous statement. "The time will come for the men [the judges] responsible for this to answer for their behavior, but not today." And Senator Bill Frist, who is a physician as well as an elected public official, stood by his diagnosis of Terri Schiavo. He had never met or examined Terri. But, after having watched a videotape of her, he stated that it was clear to him that "Based on the footage provided to me . . . she does respond."

Where did the public stand on the issue of interference from members of the executive and legislative branches of government in the work of the judicial system?

According to an ABC News poll taken on March 21, 2005, 70 percent of Americans stated that the federal government should not have entered the Schiavo case. A CBS News poll reported on March 23 that an even larger proportion—82 percent of Americans—believed that the president and Congress should have stayed out of the matter.

In the ABC poll, 67 percent of respondents agreed that the actions of elected officials had been politically motivated rather than impartial and altruistic. In other words, they felt that the conservative element in the federal government was playing to its base. The CBS poll went even further in its judgment, with 74 percent stating that the move to intervene had been "all about politics."

On the question of whether Terri Schiavo should have been allowed to die, poll results varied based on the religious affiliations of the respondents, but appeared to run between 50 and 65 percent approval. The Terri Schiavo case was a personal tragedy for all involved. Its one great public benefit may be that it spurred many Americans, regardless of their age, to prepare Living Wills or other end-of-life documents.

As a legal issue, the intrusion of the executive and legislative branches of the federal government in a state judicial matter led to a lessening of public regard for the president and the Congress and violated a basic principle of American democracy. If there was a winner in the Schiavo conflict, it may have been the Constitution of the United States.

THE CHALLENGE TO THE OREGON DEATH WITH DIGNITY ACT

Even as the Terri Schiavo case was playing out in Florida and on the national scene in the years 2000 to 2005, a challenge to the state of Oregon's Death with Dignity Act, emanating from the federal government, was building in momentum.

As previously noted, Oregon's right-to-die statute had passed the state legislature in 1994 and become law in 1997, when a bill to repeal the measure was definitively defeated by the state's citizens. John Ashcroft (governor of Missouri during the Nancy Cruzan case) was a U.S.

THe COnTROLLeD SUBSTanceS ACT anD THe BUSH ADMInISTRATIOn

As passed in 1970 and amended in 1984, the federal measure known as the CSA was designed to prevent the use of legal but powerful medical drugs from falling into the hands of black marketeers, drug smugglers, drug abusers, or to enter other illicit channels. The CSA was also intended to give the federal government control of the trafficking of illegal drugs, such as marijuana and heroin, either within states or across state lines.

It was this interpretation of the CSA that Bill Clinton's attorney general, Janet Reno, accepted. She did not see legal drugs being used legitimately under a state medical-practice law as being in violation of the CSA.

John Ashcroft and the Bush administration, on the other hand, had no way to attack the Oregon state-mandated law except through its own interpretation of the CSA, according to which the taking of drugs to commit suicide was a form of "drug abuse."

Thus, the federal law, Ashcroft decreed, was in conflict with the state law, and was in a position to preempt it.

senator from Missouri in 1998 when the Oregon act went into effect.

A longtime defender of the right to life, Ashcroft and other Republican conservatives appealed to then Attorney General Janet Reno to take action against Oregon's doctors for prescribing certain federally controlled drugs for their patients to self-administer under the terms of the Death with Dignity Act. Reno, a member of the Democratic administration of President Bill Clinton, declined to do so, finding no infringement of the Controlled Substances Act (CSA) in the practices of the Oregon physicians. For the CSA clearly permitted prescribing such drugs if they were to be used for a "legitimate medical purpose."

With the election of George W. Bush as president in 2000, a Republican administration took power and John Ashcroft became George Bush's attorney general. In November 2001, Ashcroft issued a directive to the state of Oregon, warning that, according to his interpretation of the Controlled Substances Act, aid-in-dying was not a "legitimate medical purpose" of the potentially lethal substances involved. As a result, any Oregon physician who prescribed certain drugs for a terminally ill patient (even though in strict adherence to the rules of the Oregon state law) was faced with losing his or her license to prescribe drugs of any sort.

In response to U.S. Attorney General Ashcroft's directive, also referred to as the "interpretive rule," a group of terminally ill patients and a physician-pharmacist brought suit in the U.S. District Court in Portland, Oregon, where a federal judge blocked the implementation of the directive.

The judge's opinion in *Oregon et al.* v. *Ashcroft*, announced on April 17, 2002, was that Ashcroft did not have the authority to decide what constituted the legitimate practice of medicine under the CSA and that he was intruding into a state matter. Traditionally the regulation of the practice of medicine was the exclusive province of the individual states.

Unwilling to abide by that judgment, Ashcroft then took his case to a higher court, the Ninth U.S. Circuit Court of Appeals, only to have the lower court's decision upheld in a 2 to 1 judges' verdict in May 2004. He then appealed to the U.S. Supreme Court. On February 22, 2005, the high court granted a hearing. The case was to be heard during the term beginning in October 2005.

By that time, George W. Bush had been reelected as president and John Ashcroft had left his post as attorney general, only to be replaced by the equally conservative Alberto Gonzales. The Supreme Court case, therefore, was known as *Gonzales* v. *Oregon* when it was heard on October 5, 2005.

Amicus curiae briefs were filed by groups both opposing and supporting the right to die. Conservative organizations such as Focus on the Family and the Family Research Council argued that it was appropriate in this case for the federal government to preempt state law. "Our interests are really on the moral side," said the senior legal counsel for the right-wing Family Research Council. "We believe all life has value and that a doctor's role should be to heal and not to kill."

In briefs opposed to the existence of the Oregon Death with Dignity Act, physician-assisted suicide (despite the rigid restraints and precautions of the Act) was likened to the Nazi mass murders of the disabled and the unfit, of Jews and Gypsies, in Germany during the 1930s and the 1940s.

Groups supporting the Oregon position included Compassion and Choices (formerly known in part as Compassion in Dying) and the American Civil Liberties Union (ACLU). Figures kept by the Oregon Department of

Human Services for the years from 1998 through 2004 showed that an average of thirty to forty patients a year had chosen PAS. Their deaths could hardly be compared to mass murder.

Most of those who had sought death had been terminally ill cancer patients suffering the ravages of the disease, not controllable with palliative care alone. A pancreatic cancer victim, for example, had developed mouth sores and could not swallow, became emaciated, and had fevers of 105 degrees. His death at age seventy-six, after drinking the liquid barbiturate prescribed by his doctor, was peaceful and painless.

GONZALES v. *OREGON*, U.S. 04-623

October 5, 2005, marked the third time in its history that the Supreme Court heard a right-to-die case. The first had been *Cruzan* v. *Missouri*. In its decision, rendered on June 25, 1990, the high court had recognized the right of competent patients to refuse medical treatment. It did not, however, recognize the right of incompetent patients to be represented by parents or other guardians in right-to-die matters and, in essence, it threw Nancy Cruzan's case back into the hands of the Missouri state courts, where it was finally resolved.

Justices Rehnquist and Scalia, in issuing the majority opinion, also made a strong point of asserting that it was up to the states to handle matters relating to evidence that the incompetent patient desired to die. In other words, the state was the final authority regarding medical issues, crucial and otherwise.

Once again, in 1997, individual states were given the right to decide the issue of physician-assisted suicide. In the cases known as *Washington* v. *Glucksberg* and *Vacco* v. *Quill*, which were heard in tandem, the states involved were Washington and New York. Both states banned physician-assisted suicide, and the high court's decision favored the authority of the states over federal court decisions that supported PAS and the right to die.

Even though the issue was reversed in *Gonzales* v. *Oregon* so that—unlike Washington and New York—Oregon was a right-to-die state, would the Supreme Court continue its underlying support of states' rights?

The main issue, however, was not states' rights but rather the real meaning of the Controlled Substances Act and the attorney general's authority to interpret it. While Protesters either favoring or opposing the Oregon law marched outside the Supreme Court building, oral arguments were heard within.

Justice Antonin Scalia, pursuing his ultra-conservative line of thinking, asserted that when the CSA was passed in 1970, "I would have thought that a doctor using drugs to kill a patient was unthinkable." Scalia's point was that it was time for the federal government to step in and oversee such practices as PAS.

Justice David H. Souter, on the other hand, reminded the Court that the purpose of the CSA had been to stop "drug pushers and drug abuse in the conventional sense." And Justice Ruth Bader Ginsburg raised the issue of respecting states' rights in medical matters, whether anti-PAS as in *Washington* v. *Glucksberg* or pro-PAS in *Gonzales* v. *Oregon*.

The decision of the high Court was made public on January 17, 2006. In a 6 to 3 split, the majority of the justices voted to uphold Oregon's Death with Dignity Act on the ground that it did not violate the Controlled Substances Act. The three dissenting votes came from the newly appointed Chief Justice John G. Roberts, Jr., and Justices Antonin Scalia and Clarence Thomas.

Justice Anthony Kennedy wrote the twenty-eight-page opinion for the majority. In summary, Justice

Kennedy stated that the Bush administration, via its attorneys general John Ashcroft and Alberto Gonzales, had improperly tried to pursue Oregon doctors who prescribed lethal doses of prescription medicines at the request of their patients and in keeping with the medical practice laws of the state. "It is difficult," Justice Kennedy said, "to defend the attorney general's declaration that the statute [the CSA] impliedly criminalizes physician-assisted suicide."

The judgment of the Ninth Circuit Court of Appeals—as well as the U.S. District Court in Portland, Oregon—was thus affirmed by the highest court in the land.

In a statement issued on January 17, 2006, the attorney general of the state of Oregon, Hardy Myers, wrote that, "This decision is an important victory for Oregonians. Equally important, it is a victory for patients, physicians and other caregivers in each and every state in our nation."

What would the effects of this particular instance of validation of the Oregon Death with Dignity Act be around the country?

The Supreme Court had *not* indicated in its ruling that physician-assisted suicide was a protected right in the United States. It had only affirmed a lower court's decision that Oregon physicians were not violating the Controlled Substances Act in writing potentially lethal prescriptions for the use of their patients.

Yet there is no question that states such as California and Vermont that have been trying to pass laws similar to that of Oregon were encouraged by the Court's ruling. On the other hand, a growing trend toward individual states legalizing PAS is almost certain to bring on even stronger opposition and the use of stemming tactics more potent than those employed in *Gonzales* v. *Oregon*.

How does the public at large feel about a law that would

allow doctors to comply with the wishes of dying patients who are experiencing extreme suffering in their final months of life? In a Harris poll taken in 1982, 53 percent of those questioned said that they would favor physician-assisted suicide. In a Harris poll taken in April 2005, the approval of U.S. adults jumped to 70 percent.

Various reasons are given for the marked increase in support of PAS on the part of Americans. People with serious terminal illnesses are being kept alive longer than they were twenty-three years ago, but may suffer more as a result. End-of-life matters are discussed more openly and more widely than in even the recent past. Baby boomers, a group that has learned to enjoy individuality and self-expression, are approaching their own later-life experiences.

And during the nine years from 1997 to 2006, Oregon's Death with Dignity law has illustrated how well a state-run program can work. With regard to Oregon, one important point not often mentioned is that for the relatively small number of patients who take advantage of the PAS option every year, there are many, many more in the state who derive peace of mind when stricken by serious illness.

Those patients can at least rest secure in the knowledge that help will be available to them if the time comes when they require it, thus ensuring a "good death," the true meaning of euthanasia. There is no need for them to hoard pills that may cause serious complications, to ask family members to take steps that may result in residual guilt, or to seek violent, shattering means of bringing their lives to an end.

Finally, though, there are no easy answers to the quest for a good death. While physician-assisted suicide may be available to some patients with irreversible and/or terminal illnesses, questions remain for many.

What can be done for those patients who are unable to self-administer a lethal dose of medication? In the event that no legal directives have been executed, how do we resolve the problem of the incompetent patient? Should parents, spouses, guardians, or other surrogates be permitted to speak for them?

Most seriously, how do we deal with the strongly held views in our society, both for and against, as they affect the highly personal issue of the right to die?

notes

Introduction

p. 7, "Nancy's bloated face" . . . William H. Colby, *Long Goodbye*, pp. 84–85.

p. 9, longest lived PVS patient . . . *Guinness Book of World Records*, NY: Bantam, 2000, p. 262.

p. 10, "a specific Order" . . . Colby, *Long Goodbye*, p. 50.

Chapter 1

p. 13, "a complete lack of consciousness" . . . William H. Colby, *Long Goodbye*, p. 130.

p. 13, "There may be . . . facial movements" . . . Derek Humphry and Mary Clement, *Freedom to Die*, p. 86.

p. 18, "beeping and squealing monitors" . . . Sherwin B. Nuland, *How We Die*, p. 254.

p. 20, "right of the victim to die" . . . Louis Kutner, "Due Process of Euthanasia: The Living Will, A Proposal," *Indiana Law Review*, Summer 1969.

p. 21, "considerate and respectful care" . . . Humphry and Clement, *Freedom to Die*, p. 32.

p. 24, "I didn't set out" . . . *New York Times*, Obituaries, August 4, 2005.

p. 25, "Palliative care . . ." WHO Expert Committee on Cancer Pain Relief and Palliative Care (Technical Report Series 804, Geneva, 1990).

p. 25, "life is . . . worthy of preservation without regard to its quality" . . . Colby, *Long Goodbye*, p. 269.

p. 27, "a rejection of God's sovereignty" . . . *The Vatican Declaration on Euthanasia*, Rome, March 5, 1980.
p. 27, "forgo extraordinary or disproportionate" . . . *Evangelium Vitae on the Value and Inviolability of Human Life*, Rome, March 25, 1995.
p. 27, "preservation of life . . . of paramount importance" . . . Rabbi Yitzchok Breitowitz, "The Right to Die: A Halachic Approach," *Jewish Law Articles*, http://www. jlaw.com/Articles/right.html

Chapter 2
p. 34, "Dr. Morse testified that Karen" . . . *In re Quinlan* (70 NJ 10), excerpts http://www.csulb,edu/~jvancamp/ 452_r6.html
p. 38, "Normally one is held to use only ordinary means" . . . quoted in Derek Humphry and Mary Clement, *Freedom to Die*, p. 87.
p. 38, *The Vatican Declaration on Euthanasia* . . . Principle of Proportionate and Disproportionate Means, http://www.ascensionhealth.org/ethics/public/key_ principles/ proportionate.asp
p. 40, "There is no constitutional right to die" . . . Humphry and Clement, *Freedom to Die*, p. 88.
p. 41, "respirator or life support" . . . *In re Quinlan* (70 NJ 10), excerpts http://www.csulb.edu/~jvancamp/452_r6. html
p. 42, "She was so twisted" . . . Humphry and Clement, *Freedom to Die*, p.92.
p. 43, "Although the Constitution" . . . *In re Quinlan*.
p. 43, "The individual's right to privacy" . . . *In re Quinlan*.

Chapter 3
p. 45, "The skin on her face" . . . William H. Colby, *Long Goodbye*, p. 18.
p. 48, "The testimony you will hear" . . . Colby, *Long*

Goodbye, p. 121.

p. 50, "nil" . . . Colby, p. 125.

p. 50, "required consciousness and thought," . . . Colby.

p. 51, "The abdominal area was prepped" . . . Colby, p. 157.

p. 51, "skin and subcutaneous tissue" . . . Colby.

p. 52, "Life should be cherished" . . . Colby, p. 127.

p. 52, "Unable in any manner to function" . . . Colby, p. 182.

p. 53, "If the decision's wrong" . . . Colby, p.181.

p. 54, "There is a fundamental right," . . . Colby, p. 232.

p. 56, "If she has any awareness" . . . Colby, p. 258.

p. 57, "It's reassuring that the Missouri courts," . . . Colby.

Chapter 4

p. 59, "worthy of preservation" . . . William H. Colby, *Long Goodbye*, p. 269.

p. 59, "Euthanasia, the right to die, or the right to kill? . . . Colby, pp. 281-282.

p. 61, "fed manually" . . . Colby, p. 302.

p. 70, "In sum" . . . *Cruzan* v. *Director, Missouri Department of Health* (497 US 261), June 25, 1990, Decided. http://www.law.umkc.edu/faculty/projects/ftrials/conlaw /cruzan.html

pp. 70, 72, "While I agree with the Court's analysis" . . . Colby.

p. 72, "Medical technology" . . . Colby.

pp. 72–73, "the State's abstract, undifferentiated interest" . . . Colby.

p. 73, "the possibility of subsequent developments" . . . *Cruzan* v. *Director, Missouri Department of Health* (497 US 261) June 25, 1990, laws.findlaw.com/497/291.html

p. 75, "Do you have any doubt?" . . . Colby, p. 345.

p. 75, "I think it would be personally" . . . Colby, p. 348.

p. 75, "if mentally able" . . . Colby, p. 361.

p. 76, "we would never want to be tube-fed" ...Colby, p. 335.

Chapter 5

p. 90, "Why should that decision" . . . *Washington* v. *Glucksberg* (117 S. Ct. 2258) quoted in Derek Humphry and Mary Clement, *Freedom to Die*, p. 286.

p. 90, "Isn't there the possibility" . . . Humphry and Clement.

p. 90, "Tell us what you think" . . . *Quill* v. *Vacco* (117 S. Ct. 2293), quoted in Humphry and Clement, *Freedom to Die*, p. 290.

p. 91, "All of this is in the Constitution?" . . . Humphry and Clement, p. 291.

p. 91, "this was a Supreme Court session" . . . Linda Greenhouse, "High Court Hears 2 Cases Involving Assisted Suicide," *New York Times*, January 9, 1997.

p. 92, "Our decisions lead us to conclude" . . . *Washington* v. *Glucksberg* (117 S. Ct. 2258), *Quill* v. *Vacco* (117 S. Ct. 2293), quoted in Humphry and Clement, *Freedom to Die*, p. 295.

p. 93, "A state, like Washington" . . . *Washington* v. *Glucksberg* (117 S. Ct/ 2258), quoted in Lisa Yount, *Physician-Assisted Suicide and Euthanasia*, p. 88.

p. 94, "may in fact have had a liberty interest" . . . Yount, p 89.

p. 94, "right to commit suicide" . . . Yount, p. 90.

p. 97, To obtain a prescription . . . derived from Oregon Department of Human Resources, http://www.public agenda.org/issue/fact files

p. 98, Between 1999 and 2005, 246 individuals . . . egov.oregon.oregon.gov/DHS/ph/pas

Chapter 6

p. 101, "Supreme Court Refuses" . . . Abby Goodnough, "Supreme Court Refuses to Hear the Schiavo Case," *New York Times*, March 25, 2005.

p. 104, "she apparently has been trying" . . . http://www.

usatoday.com/news/health/2005-02-25-schiavo-eating-disorder_x.htm

p. 105, "beyond all doubt" . . . Jon Eisenberg, *Using Terri*, p. 17.

pp. 105–106, "that Terri Schiavo did make statements". . . Eisenberg, p. 18.

p. 110, "In cases like this one" . . . Carl Hulse and David D. Kirkpatrick, "Congress Passes and Bush Signs Schiavo Measure," *New York Times*, Match 21, 2005.

p. 111, "Michael Schiavo is a murderer" . . . Eisenberg, p. 114.

p. 116, "don't recognize food" . . . John Schwartz, "Neither 'Starvation' Nor the Suffering it Connotes Applies to Schiavo, Doctors Say," *New York Times*, March 15, 2005.

p. 117, "build a culture of life" . . . Abby Goodnough, "Schiavo Dies Ending Bitter Case over Feeding Tube," *New York Times*, April 1, 2005.

p. 117, "The time will come" . . . Carl Hulse and David D. Kirkpatrick, "Even Death Does Not Quiet Harsh Political Fight," *New York Times*, April 1, 2005.

p. 117, "Based on the footage provided to me . . . she does respond" . . . Anne E. Kornblut, "Debate over Legislative Actions is Renewed," *New York Times*, June 16, 2005.

p. 117, "According to an ABC News" . . . http://www.abcnews.go.com/images/Politics/978 alSchiavo.pdf

p. 117, "A CBS News poll reported" . . . http://www.cbsnews.com/stories/2005/03/23/politics/main682619.shtml

p. 121, "Our interests are really" . . . Marya Lucas, "Justices are Asked to End Oregon Death Act," *Legal Times*, February 16, 2005.

p. 123, "I would have thought that a doctor" . . . Linda Greenhouse, "Justices Explore U.S. Authority Over States on Assisted Suicide," *New York Times*, October 6, 2005.

p. 123, "drug pushers and drug abuse" . . . Greenhouse.

p. 124, "It is difficult . . . to defend the attorney general's declaration" . . . News Wire Services, "Assisted Suicide Gets Supreme Nod," New York *Daily News*, January 18, 2006.

p. 124, "This decision is an important victory" . . . http://www.doj.state.or.us/releases/re1011706.htm

p. 125, "In a Harris poll" . . . http://www.alternet.org/rights/31588/?comments=view&cID=81931&pID=81869

All Internet sites were active and available when sent to press.

FurTHer InformaTion

Books

Cornelius, Kay. *The Supreme Court*. Philadelphia, PA: Chelsea House, 2000.

Fireside, Bryna J. *Cruzan v. Missouri: The Right to Die Case*. Berkeley Heights, NJ: Enslow, 1999.

McCuen, Gary E. *Doctor-Assisted Suicide and the Euthanasia Movement: Ideas in Conflict*. McAllen, TX: GEM Publications, 1999.

Patrick, John J. *The Young Oxford Companion to the Supreme Court of the United States*. NY: Oxford University Press, 1994.

Rebman, Renee C. *Euthanasia and the "Right to Die": A Pro/Con Issue*. Berkeley Heights, NJ: Enslow, 2002.

Torr, James D., Editor. *Euthanasia: Opposing Viewpoints*. San Diego, CA: Greenhaven Press, 2000.

Yount, Lisa. *Euthanasia*. San Diego, CA: Lucent Books, 2001.

_____. *Physician-Assisted Suicide and Euthanasia*. NY: Facts on File, 2000.

Statutes/Court Cases/ Documents

Bush v. Schiavo, No. SC04-925, Fla. S. Ct. (September 23, 2004)

Bush v. *Schiavo,* No. 04-757. Petition for writ of certiorari (December 1, 2004)

Controlled Substances Act, 21 U.S.C. 801 (1970)

Cruzan v. Harmon & Lampkins, CV384-9P, Circuit Court of Jasper County, Missouri (1988)

Cruzan v. *Harmon,* 760, S. W. 2d, Missouri Supreme Court, Jefferson City (1989)

Cruzan v. *Director, Missouri Department of Health,* 497, U.S. 261 (1990)

Gonzales v. *Oregon,* U.S. 04-623 (2006)

In re: Guardianship of: Theresa Marie Schiavo v. Schindler, Case No. 2D00-1269, Fla. Ct. App. 2nd Dist. (2001)

In re Quinlan, 70 N.J. 10 (1976)

Oregon v. *Ashcroft,* 192 F. Supp. 2d 1077 (2002)

Oregon v. *Ashcroft,* No. 02-35587, United State Court of Appeals for Ninth Circuit (2004)

Oregon Death with Dignity Act, Ballot Measure 16, approved (1994)

Oregon Death with Dignity Act, Ballot Measure 51, repeal rejected (1997)

Quill v. *Vacco,* 80 F. 3d 716, 2nd Circuit Court of Appeals (1996)

Roe v. *Wade,* 410 U.S. 113 (1973)

"Terri's Law," Florida State Legislature (October 20–21, 2003)

U.S. Constitution: First, Third, Fourth, Fifth, and Fourteenth Amendments

Vacco v. *Quill,* 521 U.S. 793 (1997)

Washington v. *Glucksberg,* 521 U.S. 702 (1997)

Web Sites

American Civil Liberties Union (ACLU)
www.aclu.org

American Foundation for Suicide Prevention
www.afsp.org

American Life League
www.all.org

American Medical Association (AMA)
www.ama-assn.org

Americans for Better Care of the Dying
www.abcd-caring.org

Compassion and Choices
www.compassionandchoices.org

Death with Dignity National Center
www.deathwithdignity.org

Family Research Council
www.frc.org

Focus on the Family
www.family.org

National Hospice and Palliative Care Organization
www.nhpco.org

National Right to Life Committee
www.nrlc.org

Not Dead Yet
www.notdeadyet.org

BIBLIOGraPHY

Colby, William H. *Long Goodbye: The Deaths of Nancy Cruzan.* Carlsbad, CA: Hay House, 2002.

Eisenberg, Jon B. *Using Terri: The Religious Right's Conspiracy to Take Away Our Rights.* San Francisco, CA: HarperSanFrancisco, 2005.

Fuhrman, Mark. *Silent Witness: The Untold Story of Terri Schiavo's Death.* NY: HarperCollins, Morrow, 2005.

Hall, Kermit L., ed. *The Oxford Companion to the Supreme Court of the United States.* Second Edition. NY: Oxford University Press, 2005.

_____. *The Oxford Guide to United States Supreme Court Decisions.* NY: Oxford University Press, 1999.

Harrison, Maureen and Steve Gilbert, Editors. *Life, Death, and the Law: Landmark Right-to-Die Decisions.* San Diego, CA: Excellent Books, 1997.

Hartman, Gary, Roy M. Mersky, and Cindy L. Tate. *Landmark Supreme Court Cases: The Most Influential Decisions of the Supreme Court of the United States.* NY: Facts on File, 2004.

Humphry, Derek and Mary Clement. *Freedom to Die: People, Politics, and the Right-to-Die Movement.* NY: St. Martin's, 1998.

Mauro, Tony. *Illustrated Great Decisions of the Supreme Court.* Washington, DC: CQ Press, 2000.

Nuland, Sherwin B. *How We Die: Reflections on Life's Final Chapter.* NY: Knopf, 1994.

index

Page numbers in **boldface** are illustrations, tables, and charts.

LILa PerL has published more than sixty books for young people and adults, including fiction and nonfiction. Her nonfiction writings have been mainly in the fields of social history, family memoir, and biography. She has traveled extensively to do cultural and background studies of seven African countries, as well as China, Puerto Rico, Guatemala, and Mexico. She has written on subjects as diverse as foods and food customs, genealogy, Egyptian mummies, Latino popular culture, and the Holocaust.

Two of her books have been honored with American Library Association Notable awards: *Red-Flannel Hash and Shoo-Fly Pie* and *Four Perfect Pebbles*. Ten titles have been selected as Notable Children's Trade Books in the Field of Social Studies. Lila Perl has also received a Boston Globe Horn Book award, a Sidney Taylor Committee award, and a Young Adults' Choice award from the International Reading Association. The New York Public Library has cited her work among Best Books for the Teen Age. Her most recent book for Marshall Cavendish Benchmark is *Theocracy*, in the Political Systems of the World series.

Lila Perl lives in Beechhurst, New York.